CW01597094

POETRY NOW

CENTRAL 1996

Edited by Andrew Head

First published in Great Britain in 1996 by
POETRY NOW
1-2 Wainman Road, Woodston,
Peterborough, PE2 7BU

All Rights Reserved

Copyright Contributors 1995

HB ISBN 1 85731 698 3
SB ISBN 1 85731 687 5

FOREWORD

Although we are a nation of poetry writers we are accused of not reading poetry and not buying poetry books: after many years of listening to the incessant gripes of poetry publishers, I can only assume that the books they publish, in general, are books that most people do not want to read.

Poetry should not be obscure, introverted, and as cryptic as a crossword puzzle: it is the poet's duty to reach out and embrace the world.

The world owes the poet nothing and we should not be expected to dig and delve into a rambling discourse searching for some inner meaning.

The reason we write poetry (and almost all of us do) is because we want to communicate: an ideal; an idea; or a specific feeling. Poetry is as essential in communication, as a letter; a radio; a telephone, and the main criteria for selecting the poems in this anthology is very simple: they communicate.

Faced with hundreds of poems and a limited amount of space, the task of choosing the final poems was difficult and as editor one tries to be as detached as possible (quite often editors can become a barrier in the writer-reader exchange) acting as go between, making the connection, not censoring because of personal taste.

In this anthology over two hundred and sixty poems are presented to the reader for their enjoyment.

The poetry is written on all levels; the simple and the complex both having their own appeal.

The success of this collection, and all previous *Poetry Now* anthologies, relies on the fact that there are as many individual readers as there are writers, and in the diversity of styles and forms there really is something to please, excite, and hopefully, inspire everyone who reads the book.

CONTENTS

HOW RICH AM I?

Today is my birthday, you might say so what?
Well I'm just reflecting on good things I've got
Jewels, there are many, diamonds and pearls
But none can compare with my beautiful girls
Julie and Debi, gosh how they shine!
I really feel lucky, just knowing they're mine
And who keeps my treasures all safe and sound?
The chest, in which precious things can be found?
Dave, he's my husband, lover and friend
It's his heart of gold that I'll love to the end
So I sit here today, a young fifty-four
My reflections are over, I now know for sure
Money means
            Riches, power and wealth
Treasure means
            Husband, daughters and health!

Pauline Jones

FRIENDS - LOVERS

A friend for life is a treasure to behold,
A firm hand to shake, secrets are told,
Sharing your love and sorrow too,
Making each day so perfect for you.

The days pass by with you on my mind,
A friend like you is not easy to find,
Your heart is so true, you always are there,
To prove that you love me and show that you care.

As years go by our hearts more entwine,
'I love you darling,' because you are mine,
Forever and ever our love will go on,
Our dreams we'll have cherished in love that's so strong.

Josie Simms

A PERFECT WORLD

When I awake on a summer's morning,
And see another new day dawning.
This day should be filled with untapped pleasure,
Undiscovered happiness to enjoy at leisure.
out there some day I know I'll find
The wonderful dreams now in my mind.
My world will become a peaceful place,
With laughter and smiles on everyone's face.
No-one will lack the things that they need,
As everyone else's needs they heed.
And those I love, they all will know,
They're in my heart as they come and go.
Jacky, Sarah, Fiona, Charlotte and Sue
Have my love and support whatever they do.
Karen and Suzanne, I love you so
And dream that one day, this you'll know.
Family togetherness will grow and thrive
When forgiveness and love are vibrant, alive . . .
When the whole world forgets the hating and killing,
To give friendship and love, everyone's willing.
Why can't people see this is what the world needs.
Forget wickedness, hate and unmentionable deeds.
A world with no muggings, violence or crime.
Just trust, love; forgiveness all of the time.
A perfect world we surely could make,
So let's start on it now, for everyone's sake.

Grace M Bexon

SPRING - A PROMISE

Spring is a time of colour of sweet fragrant flowers
and soft falling rain
a promise that life can be happy again

A time to reflect on loved ones gone
a promise that life will go on
a time to remember the warmth love and joy
of springs long ago when girl or boy

Cast grief aside let the sun shine through
bright spring days bring memories anew
of sadness and gladness of days long ago
the first flush of love when your heart told you so

Let your step be light let your heart be gay
cast the gloom aside for a winter's day
when the new morning sun is just a haze
think ahead to warm sunny days
when the new spring lambs jump around in the fields
think of the promise that only spring yields

Think of days in the garden with friends old and new
as the birds sing their chorus with each morning dew
live life to the full with each day given
remember you could be a long time in heaven

As spring gives way to the arrival of summer
when days are longer still
then on to autumn and colours every changing
will always bring a thrill

Though cooler now sun will still follow rain
the promise that after cold winter days
Spring will always come again

Patricia Steers

THE COLLECTION

Not of antiques, or bric-a-brac or books,
Of heirlooms handed down for looks,
But of words.
Some from schooldays, half forgotten,
Others learned, but best forgotten.
Some parsed and analysed from Latin or Greek,
or copied from others, considered elite.
Enclosed in our minds 'til needed to
Speak a thought or expression . . .
Like a professor giving a lesson.

Our mouths open up, our tongues waggle round
And out comes a sound . . .
Is it Ah or Ooh, or E, or I, or U?
Or maybe P, or T, or Zee, or R, or K or L?
Put together they'll be words,
But do we treat them right?
With respect and care?
These letters formed mysteriously?

We are careless in so many things.
Slovenly as well.
In attitudes and dress, in mind and thought and deed.
But let us not be so with words for they are very precious.
Jewels which express our thoughts, our love, our strength,
Our hopes, our fears, our innermost of wishes.
Let us with the greatest care,
Articulate, enunciate and generally pronounce
These valuable assets to our life,
Our own supply . . . of words.

Robbie Dunsmore

AUTUMN IS HERE

Tall and splendid the stately trees stand,
The wind blows the leaves upon the land,
Yellow, red and burnished gold,
Rustling and crunching as they roll.
All God's creatures great and small
Find a haven amongst them all
The hedgehog curls in a tight wee ball
All are ready for their winter sleep.
The leaves still fall - getting deep.
The sun sets low in the sky,
Billowing clouds go scudding by.
The curtains we shall draw - so tight,
Keeping out the cold, dark night.
All is peaceful, all will sleep,
Children dream of snow - so deep.
Soon it will be winter time,
The trees will sparkle with the rime.
Meanwhile all nature sleeps . . .
Until the welcome spring!

Joyce Newman

WAVE FOR DANIEL

Do you seek me wave of life?
Crashing on my broken shores,
Hissing around my feet,
Like a parent's wrath of intolerance.

In truth, that which we search for,
Remains deeper hidden than a heart in cold stone.

In love, I hide away from searing pain,
My secret walls you will not broach,
Nor tunnels to light will you dig.
I like the dark within my soul.

Richard Hearn

UNTITLED

When I first saw you, I hated you
For thinking you made the world go round.
When I first heard your voice, and you spoke to me
I hated you for being the one to make my world go round.
But when you look at me
I feel you inside my head, inside my heart
And I know it's not just air between us,
I can't breath this, it's intoxicating.
And I am no-one, but a small lost girl,
Yet in your eyes I'm whole again.
You put together the pieces
That I scattered into the wind
As I ran away from everyone and everything.
You see me as even I cannot see myself.
I think you like what you see, though I don't understand it.
Your eyes are grey,
Yet I know if I could see the world through them
It would be filled with colours
That I couldn't imagine in my dreams.
I see you with wild ponies, riding like the wind;
I see you scaling mountains and crossing streams;
I see sunsets and deserts;
Forests and oceans;
I see you soaring like a falcon
And swimming with dolphins,
And it takes me home again.

Rebecca Snape

THAT'S LIFE

Life's a bum for those who succumb
To the widening rut that engulfs every strut,
Institutions, not few, will flatter and batter you,
Get in their clutches - they'll offer no crutches,
Handle with care remains unique to glassware.
Hiccups in health, plus subsidence of wealth
Will hit one's poise, sorting *the men from the boys*,
It usually entails *going off the rails*
To return to sanity - but with dented vanity,
Some friends will astound, when misfortunes abound,
Many others soon forget, how often one met.
Survive all this, in modest marital bliss
With offspring one's proud to see in a crowd,
That hopeful start - *'till death us do part*
Will ring true till the end -
If lucky in love, with one's best friend.

Ron Jell

ESCAPE

As I glanced upon the shimmering light
Through purple sky, a dove in flight
I notice the figure of a man
Proud and upright, bold and grand
We meet, we nod, a gestured token
But as we stand no words are spoken
His eyes reveal a story of their own
They talk of torture and broken bone
And as I listen, I dare not speak
For a tear runs down his sodden cheek
A smile appears upon his face
His eyes glance up for a saving grace
Whilst overhead, the dove, wings spread flies
He dies.

Michael Langan

NORTHAMPTONSHIRE GREEN

Plants jostle by the stream,
All part of the scheme
Of things lovely, lively, loose and green.
That best of colours
Paletted for the Earth,
Mixed and matched
In this garden of great worth.
Green - in all its tints and tones,
Clothes the skeleton, the bones
Of height and form, that shape
The body on which to drape
The flower jewels: like a cape
Fastened by an invisible tape
That passes round, to and fro,
In a never ending flow
Back to more greens that grow,
That jostle by the stream,
All part of this eternal theme.

Carol McCormick

WHO AM I?

The world's a stage - or so they say
And I've had many roles to play.
Daughter, sister, sweetheart, lover
Wife, daughter-in-law, then a mother.
Niece, cousin, auntie, friend -
To this list there is no end.

Mother-in-law to my children's spouses,
Neighbour to folk in nearby houses.
Employee now and until I retire
Then pensioner until I expire!
But the role that brings the greatest joys
Is grandma to my four fine boys.

And just when I thought my list was complete
The postman came along our street
And delivered to me an envelope via
The GPO to *The Occupier . . .*
Surely somewhere there must be
A simple soul who is just *me.*

Iris P White

FUN WITH MUM

We used to have great fun
my Mum and me,
playing horses and piggybacks,
when I was three.

We used to have great fun
and roll on the floor,
chasing and catching,
when I was four.

We used to have great fun
preparing to dive,
the submarine's captain,
when I was five.

We used to have great fun
play wonderful tricks,
my Mum made me laugh a lot,
when I was six.

We used to have great fun
but now Mum's in Heaven,
and I'm sad and lonely,
not nice when you're seven.

Angela Smith

TRANSFORMATION

As I stop, relax
take a breath.
I look straight up
into the night sky.

As the cool wind
blows over me
while I look deep
into the sky
Little things like butterflies
just flutter by.

As I stop, relax
take a breath.
I look straight up
into the night sky

Yet the creatures
seem mischievous or possibly
simply devious.
As their skin changes
the wings slice skin
And their breath
leads ultimately to death.

Reverting to their natural shape
are things changing for the better
or just for the change.

As I stop, relax
take a breath.
I look straight up
into the night sky.

Robert James Haddock

PEPÉ

Do you never wonder, my lonely little Pepé,
Where are you parents? Would they
Care if maybe you were unhappy?

Do you never wonder, when you watch
The birds outside, why am I here? Could
I not join their side?

Do you never wonder what it would
Be like, to stretch your beautiful wings, and
Show them you're the king of kings.

Do you never wonder, if you would be
Given the chance, to find a lovely
Partner and enjoy a little romance.

Do you never wonder, is you whole life
To be spent behind bars? What did you do
To deserve this my Pepé? What did you
Do to deserve this?

Aalia Chaudhry

THE DYING ROOM

The door opened
I entered hesitantly
Hit by the smell of death
Touched by the feeling of fear
Yet I sensed the innocence,
And saw the last souls
Of the young dead
That once inhabited the dying room.

Nazma Begum

IMPERIAL ECHOES

This glorious land, this sceptred isle, this once respected nation
Whose sons have fought in every land and won our admiration
But, *Brit* is now a dirty word, our mighty boats are burned
Defeated foes belittle us, our royalty is spurned
Where have all the statesmen gone who made our splendid past?
And where are their successors who should have made it last?
Our Empire Days, our fleet reviews, our panoply of state
The scientists whose loss we grieve and the urge to innovate.

The words of ruination are dafter than a brush
Privatise, monetarise and cost effective slush
have swept away our heritage, not only that but more
The future of our progeny, neglected to ensure
The nation's asset strippers, without a saving grace
Are heading for the abyss with headlong lemming's pace
The last of England's miners are going on the dole
So keep the home fires burning, with lovely foreign coal.

The cars that once were British made are under foreign yoke
We bought the cars produced abroad, our factories all went broke
The Japs supply our every need in all communications
And filched the very sinews that gave us occupations
Bring back the men who gave us *Industrial Revolution*
Create the scientific means to stop the diminution
O Britain once prefixed by Great, too long dormant lain
Promote the brains and foresight to make us Great again.

Bogenschutze

EARTH AND US

The world is but a colossal head,
with seas of tears almost dead.
it doesn't think but knows the worst,
it will be gone the earth.
Our home our island out in space,
our future place of happiness.
No-one cares or don't you think,
each time you walk the street,
you're walking where trees once grew,
and concrete did not obscure the view.
The sky was once a merry blue,
and people did not cough and spew.
leave the world it's had enough,
what it needs is a bit of fuss.
Get rid of all your weapon's bombs.
Stop killing you've had your fun.
We've lost our families and our friends,
frankly sir, it's got to end.

Paula T Douglas

PASSING SHADOWS

The sun giving warmth and light
Shines out across the world
The peoples of this planet
Enjoy its warmth and beauty
Along come the rain clouds
Pushing the sun out of existence
But after the rain storms
The sun breaks through
Untarnished and beautiful as ever.

Joan Cook

MY WIFE

I sneak a private look at my wife
This lady, I have shared my life
She's not the oil painting on the wall
When stood up, she's a mere four foot tall!
Inside her soul is beauty alone,
Never do you hear her moan.
A helping hand she freely gives,
As she believes as Jesus lives!
I love to hear her gentle words,
Lord thank you for my beautiful birds.
They bring such joy into our home,
As they sing sweetly in their dome.
Please keep my husband close to me,
one day *Lord* you wait and see
He'll kneel and pray, by my side
No longer will he run and hide!
Lord send your angels down to him
As he's not ready to let you in.
I pray for the day that you will rise up
Till then, Lord, I take your bread and drinketh your cup.

Jacqui Hobbs

COUNTRY MORNING

A new day dawns over the purple hill
Trees are alive that once were still.

Birds take flight off to seek their fill
And a robin alights on my window-sill.

Above the shimmering glass of the village pond
Dragonflies hover, ducks forage in the frond.

Astir in the meadow a watchful hare is seen
From the hedgerow nesting fledglings scream.

Sheep stand grazing whilst their lambs leap high
A skylark sings in the crisp, blue sky.

Noisy cars roar down the leafy lanes
A horse bolts free from grasping reins.

The sun climbs higher, not a sign of cloud
Postie pedals past in a dusty shroud.

Morning now becomes a bustle of sound
As man and nature in tandem abound.

B Jones

TO DREAM

Slowly sank my world into a dream,
Life itself diffusing
Into mist,
I cannot see,
Slowly, oh so slowly, brushed the wind against my face,
I walk myself
Into infinity.

Turning to dock,
I can but see,
That time is non-existent in a dream.
A voice I hear?
No face it fits,
Nor hand I know,
And slowly sank my world back into day . . .
For I had only been
A dream away.

Mandy Tatum

WAR!

Knee deep in mud they stood at the front,
For King and for country they paid with their blood.
Barbed wire for miles the air full of lead,
Green pastures replaced with wounded and dead.

Fatherless children, shell-shocked old men,
Few of them speak of how it was then.

Short-sighted objectives the order of the day,
To occupy trenches a few yards away.
Dozens of lives dispensed in one blast,
This war of all wars was billed as the last.

Fatherless children, shell-shocked old men,
Few of them speak of how it was then.

Thinking of country and not of their wives,
On General Haig's orders they gave up their lives.
For medals of silver or death plaque of bronze,
A star for the few who faced death at Mons.

Fatherless children, shell-shocked old men,
Few of them speak of how it was then.

In Flanders and France they fought so well,
To end all wars they went through hell.
One service a year with a poppy for pride,
This is the way we mourn those who died.

Fatherless children, corpses of men,
None of them speak of how it was then.

S R Vincent

A MOUSE WENT TO MARKET

There was a little mouse,
Who went to the market,
And with her she took
A large wicker basket.

She bought a loaf of bread,
Some wine and some cheese,
The sun disappeared
And along came a breeze.

The breeze blew her shopping
Across the market floor,
And the poor little mouse
Had to shop once more.

She chose some heavier items,
Lest they blew away.
Tightening up her bonnet strings
She went on her way.

On her journey home,
She met a horse and cart,
Driven by a kindly gentleman
Who stole away her heart.

Now the mouse and her husband,
Go to market every week,
Children sat between them
On the horse and cart seat.

C J L Kierstenson

ARMCHAIR GARDENER

Browsing through my gard'ning books
I dream of things to come
Of velvet lawns and flowery nooks
And work as yet undone

Greenflies settle silently
As ladybirds await
Blackbirds sing in harmony
Upon the garden gate

Spiders spinning cobweb lace
To catch the morning rain
Woodlice live 'neath everything
And slugs remain unslain

A lonely beetle takes his time
Whilst caterpillars crawl
Butterflies may flutter by
But snails don't rush at all

This wildlife in my garden thrives
Amongst the many weeds
A creepy-crawly paradise
Forgives my absent deeds

Lilian Conway

THE ENDING OF CHILDHOOD

Now the day is ended,
Night has to be faced,
A substance which every
Human being is forced to taste;
Surrounded by a cage
In a vast, vast world.
Yet they say we have a choice.
They've no brains, just a voice.

Lonely souls stand alone
Fighting for the best,
Errors made, wisdom gained.
Yet pain remains within the breast,
Agony in the mind
Of a sad, sad child,
Who sees his world tumbling in,
And his life trapped in a bin.

E M Walker

JENNIE'S LAMB

Jennie had a little lamb; she nurtured it with care,
But in spite of all her nursing, it began to lose its hair.
She thought it might be lonely and company was its need,
So she found the lamb a playmate, a handsome chap indeed.

A very sexy lad was he; they called him Fred the Bear.
They played together happily, abandoned, free from care.
When Jennie went to feed them, they would coo just like a dove.
And soon it was apparent they were very much in love.

As time went by, the little lamb began to spread its girth,
And Fred would tease her gently with humour and with mirth.
One evening as the sun did set, the lamb in labour went,
And Jennie's dad, in night attire, to fetch the vet was sent.

The vet arrived, unruffled, and bade everyone keep calm
'It's going to be a normal birth, the lamb it will not harm.'
But when the baby did arrive, the vet sprang in the air.
It was a little teddy-bear completely void of hair.

When the shock was over and everyone calmed down,
Fred called for celebrations and gave out drinks all round.
He was so very proud, at last, to have a son and heir;
He did the only thing he could: he christened it Threadbear.

Eunice Ellis

THE PYRE

Oars held aloft, as we float across the dark and deep
Through the mists of vestal hue
Its folds and pleats opaque like that of the purest silk
Sliding down and shimmering across the sea

A single note from an ancient horn
Sent from the shore to herald the dawn

I command thee, curtains of mist, draw back thy veil
For she has returned to the land of her wishes
And within the flame of this pyre she will sleep forever,
beneath the ocean of her hearts delight
Never more to fear the coming of the night

A single note sent from ancient horn
Sent from the land to herald the dawn

Come now morning star shed your light
For one of true beauty leaves us with the dying of the flames
As her beauty fades from our sight so some day will your light

I stand in sadness, and plead, may her God be with her
and forever keep her by his side
If it be within his power, thought to no God do I keep
Give me the strength to weep for my wife
For she is of the pyre
And will ever be gone from my life

R Paterson

WHILE YOU STILL SMILE

Let's stop while it's still fun,
While the sun is still hot and the grass smells of hay
and I still love the way you smile at me.
Let's stop while you're still glad to hear my voice
and there's still choice.
Let's stop while the laughter is still there
and I can still stare you out, and not turn away, or beg you to stay
and you still smile at me.
Let's stop while we are still whole
and the scars on my soul will heal and not hurt me too much
and your touch can still comfort.
Let's stop while we can
a woman, a man,
together, apart, still we knew from the start this was only a part
of God's overall plan.

A Jarvis

ROMAN CANDLE

Would that I could have one moment of glory,
To fill the vaulted sky with ascension light,
Mirrored in upturned countenances.
Would that delight should stretch across the faces of the children,
And adults lose themselves in half-remembered childhoods,
Spent in the fantasia halls of ice palaces.

Would that I could be momentarily the brightest star
In an instant galaxy,
Then, lingering, fall as twinkling embers,
Lazily down to the cradling earth,
With my image still etched on the retinas
Of the ancestors of generations that will remember.

Sue Guthrie

YOUR NAME CAN STILL BE EARTH

What have we done to you?
We, the barbarians, have stripped you of your jewels,
left you bleeding in polluted waters,
defiled the beauty of your face.
We have raised ugly scars upon your body,
maimed and crippled you.
You breath, but barely so.
Your pulse is weak and slow.
Once you held close your crystal waters,
Wild creatures thrived there in abundance.
Once you breathed life into steaming forests,
they in return gave balance to you atmosphere.
Once your contours were perfect,
your skin healthy and unblemished.
Energy flowed from your whole being,
you were alive and alert,
your cheeks healthily aglow.
Not now - not now when you are dying.
Dying! - we dare not let you die!
Your death is our death!
We will learn to love and cherish you,
We will bring you back to a full life again,
heal your battered body, smooth your lumpy scars.
The gnarled and twisted can regain their beauty,
The maimed can learn to run.
We will always need you as our mother
and your name can still be Earth.

Mary Gilbey

THESE SUMMER TEARS I CRY FOR THEE

These summer tears I cry for thee,
Wash my face of sunshine caught;
Yet burn and gone, before
They touch my lips and cause me to
Cry the more.

These summer tears I cry for thee,
Are never seen;
Blown from my face by summer breeze
Afore you turn and catch
The look of love, I am forced to grieve.

These summer tears I cry for thee
You shall not know;
Shall never feel my course of love
That craves the light to blossom tiny,
In your arms; this silent longing.

These summer tears I cry for thee
Rip so my heart, are the bloods of love;
They spill as such the rains do pour
And never cease,
All summer long, they drain of me.

These summer tears I cry for thee
Are all I have to give,
And yet, you never see
Summer tears I cry
For thee.

R E Ives

THOUGHTFULNESS

An uninspiring coffee shop among
a town of ordinary dreams
Came a vision of pure excellence
that surely only I could not have seen

Youthful tall and slender,
sunlight drenching her hair
The way her body moved with laughter
pinned me to the chair

Defeating reserving weakness
I was standing close at hand
All around was meaningless -
muttered an almost decipherable sound

Slowing rising from her novel
Two deep eyes began to sparkle
Her eyebrows did the speaking
as that smile pursued the rascal

Silently back to my apartment
no greater pleasure could I find
And after our embracing glory she whispered,
'Now touch the G-spot of my mind'

Contentedly we hunger for each other
but feast at different times
My menu is mind boggling
while hers is easier to find.

Thoughtfulness between us
thoughtfulness in kind
the power of stimulation
should be explored at every find.

Graham Winwright

NEW-BORN HOPE

A single tear swept along the creases of her cheek,
Falling into the furrow beneath her nose
Into the hollow of her parted lips.
Her face was old.
It had been her only armour through the war against Time.
It was well worn.
But her eyes shone full of life
Abounding with joy.
Someone somewhere had loved those eyes,
Someone somewhere had loved that face
And remembered it as it had been.
She recalled her husband fondly.
A smile crept across her face
Smoothing out her rugged jaw.
She gazed down upon her grandson,
Cradling the child against her breast.
His face was so young.
His skin still blushing with tender freshness.
She was his guardian for the battle to come,
She was to form a shield ready for his life ahead.
She was his early strength and comfort,
He was her new-found warmth and hope.
Her tears melted in the winter firelight,
Dissolving in every soft breath of her young kin.

Natalie Usher

THE LONG HOT SUMMER

Crispy brown autumnal leaves
Crackling, crunching underfoot,
Arid pastures, scorched and barren
No serene rain from cloudless sky.

The long hot summer never ending;
People, with their buckets waiting
at the standpipes on the corner,
For that precious liquid; *Water.*

Travelling the country by-ways;
Desolation meets the eye,
Sheep and cattle standing forlornly;
Another rainless day goes by.

Come June, July . . . now late August
Is there no respite from drought?
Or is it nature's way of warning;
If you squander - go without.

Raymond Gardner

THE SILENCE IN ME

The silence in me empowers my soul
as the gentle reluctance of fate entwines its destiny.
The sodden embers, downcast by the devilment of creation,
stand defiant amongst the spearheads of enigmatic control

The euphoria of desire, lust and sacrifice lunges
desperately for sensual abandonment, as
the throng of pulverised sweetness permeates the
forgotten ecstasy of tusk-like spasms,
Self-destruct and self-denial replenish the
wanton nipple of repent.

The caveat spurns my deepest harness of internal victory
Admonishing the crusted core of flambéd jealousy.
Murmured disenchantment and vitriolic purpose, as the
velvet descent of ethereal rounds gestures a bitter longing.

PS: Your house or mine!

Sue Clapinska

STRICKEN

I cannot lose, I cannot win,
But only match the faltering steps
Down the dark demented ways of his own mind.

I seek with agonies of pain
The light of love or sound of name.
Silently, I reach to quicken
The touch of old familiar days.
But alas, no memory will ever lift
The shroud from that black abyss.

Anger burns within my breast.
Words volcanic fly unbidden, lest
Flames of passion consume
The inward self, and I
Die, little by little.

Emotion spent, my heart is filled
with deep contrition.
But down that chasm of fear
Shines light amidst the shade.
Gratitude from other hands that bless,
My child's laughter.
Her soft caress.

Irene May Collins

GRASSLANDS

Long grass swaying in the breeze
teasing
tantalising
a veil over a hidden world
stretching far across the field.
Alive
throbbing with energy
of a million living things.
Swarming insects
furtive mammals
and the school boy
in his summer hideaway
struck still by distant
parental calls at sunset.
Wishing to be alone
in the teeming throng
Unobserved.
Emperor of the grasslands.

Derek J Bacon

THE LAST FEW MINUTES OF THE '66 WORLD CUP FINAL

They think it's all over
The commentator said
Three goals to two
To the team in red
England were winning
They had the upper hand
The fever pitch crowd
Spilled off of the stand
Hurst hit the ball
And swept off his brow
They think it's all over
It is now.

Nick Alex

FEAR OF THE UNKNOWN

The darkness swallows me whole
My feet no longer touch the ground
The blood that runs through my veins
Turns ice cold
The prisoner of the dark is found
I suck in my breath
I dare not close my eyes
For the fear is too great, the fear of death
No matter how hard I try
I can't realise that I am safe
My sanity vanishes without a trace
The cold sweat trickles down my face
Grizzly sentences of torment
Play on my mind
The darkness makes me feel so small
How can my mind be so cruel
I lay paralysed to my bed
In the mirror there's nothing but red
Every inch of happiness is gone
If I dare reach out my hand
I could turn my light on
Or call mum.
No, she wouldn't understand
This just isn't me
Scared of the dark . . . I couldn't be
I can't take this anymore
I turned on the light
Just as mum opened the door
Oh, what a lovely sight!

Lindsey Robinson

BUSY WEEK, SORRY

Forgive me Lord
For I have sinned
I have neglected You
For erroneous whims.
I know imperfection
On rising each noon(ish)
Forgive me Lord
I'll remember you soon(ish).
Yes, make me remember
My roots in the carpet
Lord Your picture
is darned near perfect.

When I look on the week
And see all I have done
Lord, I can see
That You were the One
in the back of my mind;
Lord I will find
And love You again
(I hate News at Ten).

I genuflect
From seat to seat
The comfiest one
Is at Your feet
But Lord I am Home
To worship once more
Oh! Neighbours (bow head)
Is best viewed from the floor.
Forgive me Lord
You know right from wrong
My time for these questions
Is a time that's long gone
Forgive me Lord
You're darned near perfect
My odious nature

My Odious Nature
Lord *I beseech Thee!*
Was that week really worth it?

Simon Huggins

WE WANT TO BE ALONE . . . OR . . . THE GENERATION GAP

Oh Mum, you know that Roy's coming in tonight,
You said last week today would be alright.
That's right he's coming round at seven,
He'll have to leave again about eleven.
We'll play some tapes or watch TV,
I don't know what he'd like to see.
Don't make a fuss - please play it cool,
And don't shake hands - I'd feel a fool -
It's just not done these days.
I know we have some funny ways,
But times are changing . . . yes.
You'll be just fine in that blue dress.
When you and Dad go out, please slip away
In quite a normal, casual way.
Don't act all coy
In front of Roy.
Oh Mum of course we'll be alright,
He isn't staying overnight.
Don't worry - there's a pet,
We've hardly kissed each other . . . yet.

S R Ramsden

INSECTICIDE

Why is it that I can't kill insects?
The wood louse trundling across my bathroom floor
I could no more
Crush him than boot off the head
Of that angelic child next door.
Nor stamp on the blistering eye and gangling legs
Of Arachnid, the spider,
Villain of my seedling days.

What stops the swot that kills the fly
To send him gently buzzing free?
That saves the severing of a chain
Of ants intent on banditry?
Lure them with sugar,
Turn them about,
But kill them?
No, it's not for me.

Why is it that I can't destroy
These predatory pests
Who bloat themselves, spew out their mites,
Invade my deepest privacy?

Is it the force that drives the sea,
That drives the ant, the wood louse
And drives me?
Encompassed in that lightning field
Fissioned by dynamic power,
The cells within us jetting sparks.
Extinguish one.
Diminish all.

Hazel Crutchley

SECOND CHANCE

Our Planet that was raped and burned,
cried out, 'Will they never learn?'
But Everyman just said, 'This isn't really my concern.'
And so the mother earth did bleed,
her spirit crying in her need.
Her forests that were stripped away,
her poisoned oceans, that hid decay.

The spirits of the stars did hear, the crying of their sister Gia,
they came to heal her wounds and mend,
the ravages of wicked men.
Then the mighty paw of God,
smote Man, from the planet's sod,
and laid him low, and let him see,
the things that they have wrought on thee.

The thunderclouds did roll and peal,
and lightning forked, and stabbed, and reeled.
The oceans rose, and rain did pour,
and quenched out all the human sore.

But in her pity, Earth did plead,
to save a few, to save the seed.
And so the mighty paw of God, did stay,
from casting everything away,
and gave another chance to Man,
another season, another plan.

And so Atlantis, proud and tall,
sank deep within the ocean's maw,
but will we learn from their mistake,
or is it even now, too late?

Len Lewis

HELPING OUR WAY

My grandsons came to stay a while,
I must admit they made me smile,
Can we help? Grandma they said,
Imagine the thoughts that went round my head.

I decided to make the housework fun,
As one job after another was done,
The washing up water was a lake,
The boats were cups, saucers and a plate.

The legs on the table were the next call,
As on their knees they did crawl,
They came up gleaming with polish so bright,
My grandsons too were such a sight.

The Hoover a nice snake did make,
As across the jungle its way it did take,
I don't like snakes was my cry,
As the Hoover went wriggling by.

The bedroom was the next port of call,
As on my knees I was ready to fall,
The sheets made a friendly ghost,
But I enjoyed the pillow fight the most.

The bath an ocean liner did make,
As around the world, our journey we did take,
The taps turned on were high tide,
As water down the plug hole did glide.

Helping each other had been fun,
As through each task we worked as one,
It's a pity that the world cannot see,
That helping is better than fighting will ever be.

R Lee

TWO SIDES TO THE COLOUR RED

Red Cross helps, red tape doesn't.
Red Arrows in the sky, Red Indians on the ground.
Red pepper for vegetarians as no red meat allowed.
No Red Carpet, when red carpet shown.
Account in the red, so red bus ride home
How shall I send a message? Red phone or pillar box.
Hot red embers can cause a fire - big red engines will put it out.
A man might be red-faced if seen in a red light district
After seeing red, will the lady accept a red rose?
It was a red letter day until I *red* about the tragedy.
A crafty red slipped in says the snooker player.
Are you *red'y* for a question?
Does a red admiral salute when he sees the red ensign?
To finish with - take a complimentary glass of red wine
but don't allow it with you, red blood if driving
Because you might see a blue light.

Stephen Parkinson

THE NIGHT

When the day has ended
the sun bids us goodnight.
The moon does show his face to us
and darkness comes the nights.

A thousand stars do watch us
as to bed we go.
and as our sleep becomes us
the seeds of dreams we sow.

The world it does surrender
to the stillness of the night.
Time is at a standstill
until comes morning light.

Maggie Prickett

THE VISIT

Who was that old man dressed in white?
I met him in my dreams last night.
He shrieked and snarled outside my door
A hundred rats crawled across the floor

He wore dead cow skin around his feet
This claw-like hand reached out to greet
He dragged me screaming from my bed
Blood pumped fear around my head

I was trapped inside a cold embrace
The flesh dripped from his rotting face
He bared his teeth or what was left
With eyes on fire he screamed . . .

I am Death!

Jake Baker

UNTITLED

Feel my body, soft and smooth,
Run those hands, till I approve,
Smell the fragrance of my skin,
Feel this love, that flows within,
Hold your body, close to mine,
Make it move, with mine, in time,
Touch me now, my body waits,
To be apart, is what I hate,
Feel me now, and touch my heart,
Closer now, and never part,
Our bodies melt, and we are one
Feel my senses, till they're gone,
Let me hold you, one more time,
Because tonight, you're only mine.

Marilyn Wright

EVERYONE'S A WINNER

A faceless man in the public eye
A semi-detached house
A deserted home just a car on the drive
A billionaire's paradise.

A gold-paved route to happiness
A fragile list of terms
A fortune beyond one's wildest dreams
A seething can of worms.

An unholy quest for the Holy Grail
By Camelot spurred on
An opening of Pandora's box
Eclipse of the rising sun.

Harem condemned by the Holy Koran
A miserable sinner
A worshipper at Mammon's shrine
Doubts *everyone's a winner.*

Ray Wilson

ALLSLOPS FABLES

People who live in glass houses should draw their curtains at night.
The grass is always greener on the other side, especially if you live in a flat.
A fool and his Mummy are soon parted.
A rose by any other name is probably some other flower.
Better the devil you know than the blonde girl in the Co-op.
Beware the Ides of March, and the Smiths of Ely.
One good turn deserves a mother.
All comes to him who waits but who wants to be a waiter?
Never put off till tomorrow what you can do next week.
Make Kay while the sun shines, she might not like the cold.
An apple a day keeps the Doctor away, an onion a day keeps everyone away.

H E Weeks

UNPLANNED (1995)

I didn't mean to walk this way again,
The cancer path of nineteen ninety one.
I stood my ground defiantly back then
And turned from greying shadows to the sun.

But here I am - I've seen them all before:
Reception's chic, detached, efficient crew,
The nurse with gentle, reassuring jaw
And eyes that wondered just how much I knew.

We thin-robed patients, each an isle of dreams,
Are not yet bonded by a verdict shared,
For who can tell behind the magazines
Which ones will feed the daisies or be spared?

This doctor, concentrating on his task,
Still wears the immortality of youth
And, fearing probing questions I may ask,
Rehearses softly how he'll tell the truth.

Relax my friend, we know the likely score:
We're past the stage of horror and surprise:
And some of us have done it all before;
So take a breath and look us in the eyes.

We'll show you our achievements yet to come,
For every hour we use is bonus time,
And every smile and every plan begun
Convinces us that this is still our Prime.

Let's decorate the path with cherished schemes
And walk through love and laughter every day,
For greying shadows feed on dying dreams -
- which cannot die until they're thrown away!

Jenny Whiteside

SELF

Some take time to put the ragged dress
Of this egocentric self aside,
And see the struggle of their contending parts.
But fashion's acolytes careering
Through clouds of profit and pride
Doggedly deny this notion of another self.
That other self, disowned and despised,
Rises up in a blinding fury of despair
And topples down all the stones ambition assiduously heaped.
Thought becomes archaic in a gilded age of youth,
An unruly abode of boors and brigands
Where chaos parcels movement by fits and starts.
The unholy place of wilful savagery
Where inexperience must learn to decipher
The babble of fools and devil's disciples,
And choose between self-pity and self-appraise.
Some see fit to make amends,
Retrieve that time lapse lost
And have the wit to let that alter ego reign.
They build anew a nobler structure
To house their loving harmonies,
Finding a nearer paradise than they could know.
But most rush on to accolades of fantastic farce,
Waylaid by roars and echoes
Of an enfeebled ego's wanton whim.

Robert Hendon

PANE

I am broken into a thousand pieces
Razor edged and crystal hard
Each shattered shape a tiny mirror -
a crazed and splintered glass shard.

Reflecting colours, yet colourless.
Empty as a hollow heart
a falling chandelier of teardrops
tinkling in the growing dark.

On the bare and dusty floor I lay
In the deepening gloom
Helpless, hopeless and alone
In that old forgotten room.

The cold moon glints through grimy windows
Watching me with its baleful stare
Till I sink into eternal darkness
And intolerable despair.

J A Boyle

HOPE

Late at night
cobbled streets of light
As the rain falls down
on this lonely town,
I hide away.
Fearing another day,
I've tried so hard
I don't need pity
Just a chance to
leave
My cardboard city.

Kate

PREMONITION

Just stare into my eyes
There should be no surprise
Only the reassuring proof
Of my sincerity and the truth
I could demonstrate all my different feelings
Though words and actions are prone to misunderstandings
Let us just sit here calm and accept each other
As we are human imperfect and peculiar
This moment is ghostly and lovely
Like the merging of past and future memory
Let us live today for now is delightful and extraordinary
This is the first time we have met but strangely
My soul is in love with you I cry about you silently
Inside through wanting to be everything for you forever
And wishing that we could always be together.

Stephen Neal

ALZHEIMERS

I look deep into your dear face.
And clasp you in a warm embrace.
You don't know me anymore, and so
The tears inside me seem to grow
I must not release them yet my love
But pray for strength from Heaven above
So my dear Husband, Lover, Friend
I will always love you to the end
I'll never more hear you whisper low
'My dearest dear, I love you so.'
Illness has claimed you in its grasp
And all your memories dwell deep in the past

Constance Gayton

SLUMLAND

Slumland in the middle of spring
no birds sing
as if a bird perched in the gutter
could be heard above the wind
no it would be just a mutter

mutter it doesn't matter
it hardly matters

seldom do we hear
a bird singing here
but once - just once
I saw a sparrow alight
upon a rooftop
her feathers all torn
- a broken wing
slumland, no birds sing.

David A Simon

WE ALONE

Sometimes all the reasons seem madness
Yet there is light in the darkness that flows
We alone know our balance of sorrow and joy
We alone know the end of our growth
We alone can decide on our destiny
We alone choose the sunrise we see
We alone cast off our hell for a heaven
Unrestrained, liberated, free.

Simon Paul Rooney

NEVER TALK TO STRANGERS

Children do be careful
While you are out to play
Don't talk to any strangers
Or wander far away
Always tell you parents
Exactly where you're going
And *please* don't go with anyone
Without your parents knowing
Never talk to anyone
Though friendly they may seem
Turn, walk away and say *no,* to sweets
Or the offer of ice-cream
Never play out after dark
It's *dangerous* at night
Never go off on your own
To places out of sight
Don't get in any vehicles
With a friend or on your own
Remember also if you can
Always take the safe route home
If a stranger does approach you
Report it immediately
To a member of your teaching staff
Or your family
Although during your lifetime
You will meet many, many dangers
Please while you're young *remember*
Never Talk to Strangers!

Kathleen A Clarke

ODE TO MR STIPE

When seagulls have a meeting
What do they discuss?
Spacemen on your mantelpiece
Polar bears named Gus.

Do some laugh at vampires
Who eat stale cherry cake
Tear tissue into ribbons
Fight with hoe and rake

Others may like grunion runs
On pink beads wish to sail
Sneak up on a ginger cat
Don't peck or pull its tail

The get-together over
Seagulls in a heap
Watch re-runs of blossom
Then drift off to sleep.

Nikky Ingram

HOUSEWIFE'S LAMENT

I don't care if the world is round,
I don't care about the failing pound,
I don't care about my saggy bum,
Marshmallow tits and sticky out tum.

Nothing matters any more,
You do your best they just want more,
Do this, do that, be a good mother.
Your only reward is a bit of the other.

Gas bill, mortgage, life's too short.
Self-esteem just can't be bought.
I need more than a play on the telly
And a corned beef sandwich from down the deli.

I want fun, I want money.
I want a guy who'll call me honey
A yacht in the bay would be quite nice
And a few million quid on the roll of a dice.

I want gold, I want sun,
I want an op to lift my bum.
I want a miracle from up above.
But all I really want is *love!*

Andrea Clarke

WALKING TALL

I had to shave and now I am bare
An injection here and an injection there.
This won't take long, I'll feel no pain,
Lying on my back - will I be the same?

No boxer shorts to wear for a while
NHS briefs bring relief and a smile.
Do drive slow and watch out for those bumps.
Gently my dear, please think of my lumps.

My hair is growing and I need some cream,
They itch real bad - I'm going to scream.
An ostrich egg they've swollen to size
My word but they're big, and I've two black eyes.

Well I'm feeling frisky, over here my sweet,
I love you dearly, come give me a treat.
I need to know, I must be sure
That what I've got will work once more.

Now don't joke lads, don't be so cruel
For this could happen to your tool.
And so you guys be nice to me
For what I've had is a vasectomy!

Krystyna J Nicholls

UNIQUE RAIN

I think I'll write a poem,
Unique in every way,
Thinking words of clever talk,
Perhaps will make my day,
But try as hard as pen can write,
And thinking but in vain,
I look outside for something new,
And all I see is Rain,
The sky is oh so gloomy,
The clouds not good to see,
Then in a flash it happens,
The poem comes to me.
Rain the need of all our souls,
A lovely falling joy,
Without it life would never be,
For every girl and boy,
Unique - a gift from way up high,
Our hearts to quench and free,
The wondrous joy of heavenly rain,
Is there for you and me.

Phyllis Audrey Callow

BIRTH

A sterile room, a trolley, a chair,
Nagging wives with words of wisdom
'Screaming won't do you any good,'
An every-day event for them.

Weary, tired of pushing and panting,
Bewildered yet excited of the time ahead,
Stale sweat, a blood stained dress,
On a high with gas and air,
Mopped brow is hard to bear.

You enter the world like a champagne cork,
All eyes peer at the skinny rabbit,
Blue and deformed with an egg-shaped head,
A scrawny wail for the breast of its mother.

A weigh, a bath and then a reunion,
A count of the tiny fingers and toes
Perfect, a stitch or two, a cup of tea,
Then a slow walk back to the ward.

D J Horne

REFLECTIONS

You sit and think, at least you say you do,
And yet, when standing quietly by and watching you
I wonder - so young you are untouched by pain
You child, you lovely child set in your woman's frame.

You sit and think and sweetness is thy grace
Ere now untouched, yet looking to life's face
With candid eyes your gaze unspoiled by twists of fate
Whose tendril coils lie waiting to acclaim you for its mate.

You'll sit and think and think again along those tender years
When life's strange path unfolds itself, reveals your hopes, your fears.
And fate will take you by the hand through soaring heights of ecstasy
And many vales of tears.

You'll sit and think and think yet more all through those further years
Which lead from youth to middle age, when life's sweet debt is in arrears
The mirror of your life will then before your eyes unfold
And you may say God bless the day my destiny was yet untold.

So lovely child as years go by perhaps you'll sit and think again
And when you are old and tired and wise
Your inner voice may quietly say
I'm glad I was a child upon that lovely summer's day.

Elizabeth Oliver

NONENTITY

I am here,
This is me.
Look around and you'll see
I exist.
Well, I think . . .
Yes, I *do*.
I've seen me,
I know.
Just look harder,
I'll show you
I'm here.
Someone once said 'Hello!'
And I think they were talking to me,
Let me see,
It was only a few months ago.
Then, again, there were quite
A few people that night,
Who were milling around to and fro.
So it could be I'm wrong,
Though the feeling was strong
That I had a real identity;
But perhaps it was just
A vain hope, that I must
  Be a person,
    A someone,
      A me.

Sheila O'Neill

STORIES HE WOULD TELL

When I was a little girl
My Dad would tell me stories,
Of big black witches that flew around
On their broomsticks through the towns.

They would frighten all the children
And the cats and dogs would hide,
The curtains were always drawn at night
So they couldn't see inside.

But one witch was always daring
My Father used to say,
She would sneak up to the kitchen door,
The lock had broke that day.

Through the house she would go
To find unsuspecting children,
Dreadful things would happen
If she found one that was sleeping.

But then he'd change the story
Everything would be alright,
My Dad was behind the kitchen door
To give the witch a fright.

He stood with a jug of water
To put over the witch's head,
For then she would disintegrate
At last she would be dead.

My Dad became my hero
By the stories that he told,
Stories that I would remember
Until I am very old.

Carol James

YOUR GHOST

Your ghost forces crystals through my
Tears burn like rivers of lava
Searing the vista of my
Hope withers as I beat my ragged fists
Against my own bloodied chest
Heaving a sigh, my shaking hand wipes my
Face the music, face facts
Your face tattooed across the sere skin of my
Heartfelt emotions clumsily expressed -
A five year old diamond cutter,
St Vitus neurosurgeon,
A whoring priest . . .

I stammer through this,
My final dramatic oration,
Unsure whether to weep.
(Too theatrical?)

I look up from my tattered notes to find the audience gone,
Like smoke dispersed,
And the theatre empty,
Save for the wide open and laughing mouths of the red velvet seats.

I take my bow.

M A Cox

TO CHARLOTTE

An angel once graced me softly,
I wept;
Tears of beauty cascaded my cheeks,
For human eyes were not meant to contend
With such divine purity,
Deep Spanish eyes with flowing locks,
Mahogany skin and soft postcard lips.

Her presence hynotised my foolish gaze
With a cathedral-like sanctuary,
Her touch was warm and knowing:
As our lips sank,
We became one and radiantly glowed,
As angels often do.

I will never forget my Charlotte,
Her elegant persuasion
Still dances magically within
The velvet chambers of my heart,
As I flutter my quill in quiet desperation
I caress the tears from my eyes,
As an angel did once.

Simon Booy

OUTCASTS

You ask me why? The eyes beneath the unkempt hair
Grew weary, his voice was rough, 'As if you really care'
Clutching the empty bottle, he drained the evil smelling dregs
And hurled it at the wall, I saw his trembling legs
Give way, as falling on the ragged bed
He fumbled in his pocket, and looking at me said
'I am one of hundreds, meths, drugs, the lot
Misfit, outcast, layabout, a broken, drunken sot
Your modern world, society, turns from me in distaste
Do-gooders shake their heads, and whisper 'Oh dear, what a waste.'
He laughed, his pallid features creased in silent mirth,
I felt that I was looking at the loneliest man on earth,
The box-like room was stifling, the filth beyond endurance
I turned to go, but was held by the searching perseverance
As shaking fingers emptied pockets, I waited - at a loss
The hand withdrew, and silently, held out the
Victoria Cross!

Irene Hustwait

NIGERIA

We had servants galore,
Who could ask for more,
We came to make our fortune.
And in less than a year,
Eaten away by loss and fear,
We left my father's homeland.

The orange earth, the bright blue skies,
The golden sparkle of fireflies,
At night, when life seemed magical.
The coups, the murders, so many dead,
A man found with a machete in his head,
The sudden shock of my father's homeland.

The damp, sticky heat that lingers,
The delicious stews we ate with our fingers,
Hot and spicy to make you sweat!
King Sunny Ade and his African Beats
Played one of the rhythms to which I moved my feet,
The heartbeat of my father's homeland.

My uncle's fingers, covered in rings,
His mansion filled with beautiful things,
I didn't know my family was rich,
My grandmother's tiny, iron-roof shack,
Filled with my cousins, nameless and black,
What is this place? My father's homeland?

A land of broken promises and dreams,
It left its mark on us, or so it seems,
I see an invisible scar on each of us.
We packed our bags and said goodbye,
And none of us knew how to cry,
As we left my father in his homeland.

Rachel Lisboa

CURL

Like an absolute saint
A wide-eyed grin
Says a lot to me
Mud on my chin
Toe tapping shyness
Knock knees grazed
Finger inside a mouth
And sways.

Cheeks flushed
A ruddy redness blush
Zip goes up and down
Head scratched
Shirt sleeve twisted
Around and round
Stares at the floor
Then quickly looks up
To see if you saw.

But if you can't see
Then neither can they
It's an innocent game
And I have to play
With only one shoe on
Bicycle gone astray
I'm a loveable rogue
In May

Neil Wadey

RAGE

What is this thing called *Rage,*
That turns sweet face into very old age,
It starts insidiously slowly,
Taking away serenity and all that's *Holy.*
Building and bubbling inside my head,
The colour of face and neck turned red,
With heat churning stomach and shivering thigh,
Steam of anger shows through eye,
Smells and tastes like sulphur vapour,
Feels like brittle touchlight taper,
Words tumble out of tight-lipped face,
Screeching from throat at a thrashing pace,
Tone getting louder ready to explode,
Like writhing snake and springing toad,
Dashing out of widening mouth,
Toward once friend, now shivering mouse.
Until at last the *Rage* is spent,
My mind and heart is duly rent,
I try to repair the outside thatch,
Of head and face with smiling patch.
But all is lost I cannot mend,
The hurt and hand of my friend.

Trish Birtill

SWANS

Swans are majestic, serene and white,
They glide through the water in dreamy moonlight,
Elegant long necks in effortless flight,
Unless fisherman's lead weights they painfully bite,
Help them we must in this awful sad plight,
This form of pollution we all must fight,
If we don't want to lose this beautiful sight,
It is our pleasure, heritage and right,
To have lovely white swans to admire with delight.

Margaret Hooton

FORGIVE AND FORGET

Worried about the way he feels about me,
Upset about what I've said,
I only hope he can see
it was a mistake I made.
I want to tell him I'm sorry
but I don't know what he feels,
I just want to see him happy.
I wish it was that real.
He's been angry with me
ever since it happened,
but I don't think he himself
has realised he's that saddened.
I love him with all my heart
and that's why it hurts.
To see him in pain
is the last of my wants.
I can't ask for his forgiveness,
lately, that's all I've been after
but I want to apologise,
for having stopped laughter.
Getting back to the way we were
will be a little difficult,
but I hope we can soon get there
because I want to let him know how much I care.

Shahena Begum

THE MAYFLOWER

This is the Hawthorn's wedding day -
For she wore a dress of virgin white,
Carefully layered at her boughs.
And as her branches swayed in the breeze,
She made her Springtime vows.

Let the humble bumble bee wed me to,
The handsome well-groomed earth.
So nurturing all my spreading roots,
Amongst riches of my woodland church.

And as her branches swayed in the breeze,
She made her springtime vows.
Providing the everlasting infinity,
Where I will flourish and remain.

To pay homage to a host of guests,
Of feather and fur.
In the house of your green domain,
Planting my garden with flower upon flower.

For she wore a dress of virgin white,
Carefully layered at her boughs.
And as her branches swayed in the breeze,
She had, made her Springtime vows!

A E Carr

UNTITLED

Deep within the fields that lay behind the housing estate on which I grew up, lie the secret places of my childhood. Where in my youth, I would run and laugh, although quite alone. I'd sit by the canal side and dream up new worlds, or make-believe the spinney was a huge forest in a fantasy land of warriors and magicians.

Now I have grown and moved on, into the material
world of buses and Friday nights down the pub. I work
hard and spend money. I have friends and lovers.

But in my mind, the grass of those fields still shifts
with a late summer wind, and the canal water still rushes
through the lock, and the child that was once me
runs through that spinney, dreaming, pure and happy.

Fred-E

MEMORIES OF A CORBY HIGHLAND GATHERING

Massed pipe bands in full array
Salute their Chieftain on parade
Blaw *Helin Laddie* chanters strain
Chieftain salutes their loud acclaim

Highland dancers two hundred strong
Traditional dances danced all day long
Pipe bands play to win the fray
Top solo pipers Piobroch play

Drum Major strides flourishing mace
Judged on marching style and pace
To caber tossing strong men flock
Winning caber strikes twelve o'clock

Massed pipe bands in full array
Salute their Chieftain at end of day
Blaw stirring *Green Hills of Tyrol*
A thrilling sound a Scottish sound

Making my way to my abode
Fond memories keep as I grow old
Of kilted Chieftain proud and bold
Twenty thousand to the Gathering strolled

John L Douglas

STEPHANIE

She has left - again!
I should be used to her coming and going.
She came back before,
The ache should be less with the knowing.

It's a sign you've done well, so people tell.
You've given her the confidence to fly.
But the house is so bare, her clutter not there;
And I just want to sit down and cry.

Although I am sad - for her I am glad;
It means my work has not been in vain.
So I put a smile on my face, and fix it in place,
Hoping one day she'll come home again.

A child yesterday, a young lady today,
Who now knows the answer it seems;
To the 'Why? Mummy why?' Once endless times cry,
Now an echo that haunts me in dreams.

But a tap or a knock, a key in the lock,
And a smile coming in through the door.
With a bag full of laundry, a heart full of love,
And my house is a home just once more.

She has left - again!
I'm getting used to her coming and going.
She is only a few miles away,
I do feel better for the knowing.

Wendy J Wearing

THE SEA

What is the sea
for the mystery it holds
there are so many
which are untold

The treasures buried so deep
are a real danger to seek
the glittering gems
that once were worn

From the beautiful clothes
which are now so torn
the sound of the waves buried deep
of our memories to keep

The sea is our lifeline
to bring and go
for the food we eat
which some countries can't grow

The sea is a beautiful sight
when ships sail in the darkness of the night
with their different lights glowing
with the different ways they are going

But one thing is certain
we all must know
that Jesus walked on the sea
so many years ago

And the multitude he fed
with two small fishes
and five loaves of bread

It is still a mystery
and always will be
from now until Eternity.

E Warren

WILD AND FREE

My home is so cosy, and warm and compact
My garden is landscaped with hills and a track
Where wild flowers grow in abundance so sweet
Poppies, daisies and buttercups all meet

My neighbours, the squirrels, hedgehogs and bunnies
At one with nature, like bees and honey
Trees and pastures on warm summer days
Romping in fields of corn and maize

No worry of bills, or mortgage and cars
I live my life happily under the stars
My job is to help Mother Nature ensure
This planet stays clean, and green and secure

Babbling brooks, and warm summer meadows
Cotton wool clouds and lush green hedgerows
Rambling through woods with the wind in my hair
I'm free as a bird without worry or care

My conscience is clear, my spirit is free
Without the bounds of hypocrisy
No stress, no strain, no worries or cares
There's nothing on earth which nearly compares

You too, can join in this venture for perfection
And look back on life with a better reflection
I cherish my life, which is wild and free
A Romany life is the only one for me.

Loretta C Searle

REMEMBER THE CHILD

Ferrari, lipstick red
In the showroom, chrome
Flattering eyes back
Distorted, head squeezed
In its compound curve.

Mind avoiding its details,
Fixed on the whole, the
Ideal of speed in the
Sunshine; wearing its
Second skin mentally.

Feeling its pulse
Echoed back from shop
Windows, blank with recession;
Dreaming its way up
Out of the worn shoes.

Hands on the wheel
Of the mind; squealing its
Tyres with a toe flick,
Feeding its engine's adrenalin
Into the pavement.

Escaping the grid
Lights, free in its own
Wind: leaving the following
Eyes in the mirror;
Aimed at the open sky;

King in the head.

W B Skinner

INSPIRED

(Dedicated to Gill Lockart)

This lovely soul of wisdom full
Transfers this on to I
Releasing lots of binding thoughts
Through emotions that we cry

Release into the universe
Thoughts filled with sullen gloom
Accept from her sweet words of Strength
While calm fills up the room

An angel sweet, sure sent from Heaven
No more perfect could you find
She makes you laugh and she makes you cry
As she heals your troubled mind

She is so special in a caring way
Her soul shines through her eyes
Take heed of what this angel says
Because she is wisdom full and wise

The caring that this lady gives,
Nothing can ever measure
When *Gill* was born into this world
Heaven lost its greatest treasure

Sylvia Armer

LITTLE DOG

Little dog, coat black and white
What do you do from morn till night?
When I'm far away at school,
Do you keep your master's rule?

Go you off the streets to roam,
Paths and by-ways far from home?
When your master's far away,
What do you do all the day?

Little dog, I'll soon be back,
With my satchel on my back,
And I know you will not fail
To greet me with a wagging tail!

John Woolley (13)

BIRDS' FINAL PLIGHT

Where do all the dead birds go, where do they lay?
Somebody asked me the other day.
The answer to me is as clear as a bell
Don't you know it? Can't you tell?

When their times comes they soar through the sky
Straight up to Heaven . . . and then they die.
For they're practically angels already, I feel,
With lightness of feather and song ethereal.

And God lays them gently on pillows of cloud
Embalms them with love, no need for a shroud.
And when it next rains to freshen the air
You'll know that the spirits of birds will be there.

For the clouds will break up to let the sun shine some more
And the birds will rejoice for their fellows before.
So wonder no further on birds' final plight,
They forever are singing,
Forever in flight

Diane Davis

PLASTIC JOCK

I was born in Kettering hospital
But I think I'm a Jock,
I keep a can of Irn-Bru
Down my tartan sock.
My family hails from Glasgow
Of that I'm really proud,
I'd like to go and see them
But Mum says I'm not allowed!
When I go for a pint
I pull on my Ranger's shirt,
And when I go to weddings
I wear my little skirt.
I really get annoyed
When people say to me
'You're not a proper Scotsman, . . .'
They simply cannot see.
Yes it's true I've never breathed
An ounce of Scottish air,
And yes I 'd find it difficult
To find my own way there
But . . . I've got my kilt, my sporran
And my tam o'shanter too,
I'm born and bred in Corby Town
But I'm Scottish through and through!

Dean Sheldon

FOR YOUR WEDDING DAY

May the sun shine brightly in your heart and last your whole
lives through,
May the rain and snow stay far away from everything you do,
Let the breeze sing in your garden accompanied by the larks,
And let rainbows glow above our home to keep away the dark.

For your love is like a fairy tale, a picture book come true,
But this isn't the end of the story, it's just the beginning for you,
And every day that passes, a new page will be turned,
With love and life and happiness and lessons to be learned.

You are two special people that radiate with love and fun,
And your lives will be a beautiful story now that you are joined
As *One*

Cheryl Anderson

BENJI

He's only a crossbred I know,
No medals he'd win in a show,
But his dear little face really wins him first place,
In my heart, 'cos I love him so.

We are great pals, him and I,
Will remain so till one of us die,
We share walks together in all sorts of weather,
He loves it, that great little guy.

He likes playing games with a ball,
I throw it to him along the hall,
He will never grow up, he's still like a pup,
Though full-grown, but still very small.

He understands all that I say,
Knows just what I'm doing each day,
And at night while I'm sleeping, he's alert and is keeping,
A watch over me, come what may.

He's the best thing that's happened to me,
And when he climbs on my knee,
The love in his eyes is truthful, no lies,
He's all mine, my little Benji.

M Garrett

WOOTTON - PROFIT AND LOSS

On a sunny southern hillside,
In the rolling Midlands country,
Lay an unpretentious village,
Known to Saxons, Vikings, Normans
As the farmstead in the forest.
There the people lived by farming,
Lived to plough the open furlong,
Raise their stock and bear their children.
Thus they lived as humble toilers,
Never moving from the hearthside
Of their forebears and relations;
Knowing those who lived beside them,
Knowing all the village people.
So it was for countless ages,
Only changing with the seasons,
With the sowing and the reaping,
With the ploughing and the harvest;
Till the horse gave way to engines
And the dusty roads were metalled.
Then the town reached out about them,
Swallowed up their fields and byways,
Took their land, their flocks, their cattle
And built houses in their pastures.
People came from far off places,
Came and settled in the houses,
And their neighbours worked in cities,
Came and went as unknown strangers
In a land of bricks and mortar.

Rosemary D Joll

ANOTHER

Another song, another time,
Another man in these arms of mine.
Will it ever stop?

The sun came out and touched his hair
And I knew. It would reflect there,
Until he moved.

The baby lay, not far away.
And all I wished, was to be far away.
And then. The guilt came.

Women women everywhere.
You are free *now*.
It is in print. It must be true.

Work you now, for hard fought pay.
Then home.
Your home to play.

When finished.
You may polish off at bars
You will have paid.

You can with care. Have it all.
You can with care. Ride any storm.
But who cares?

Marysia Riley

WAKERLEY WOODS

Do you remember? A sunny
May day, we walked the
Woods of Wakerley Clay.
Bracken fronds, whispering
Pines, orange flowered cones,
Newly green spines

We laid on our back in
Grass, lush verdant green,
Looking up at the sky with
Its heavenly scene
Trees of all one, burgeoning power
Ever upward, together, closer,
Life's final hour
            Do you remember?

Hoof trails of horses, embedded
Paws of dogs, yellow archangel
And pine scented logs.
Who found the hod-me-dod
Shell? So perfectly formed
And coloured as well, the
Bleached rabbit skull, and
Who made a spell?

Sounds of birds, the call of
The pheasant, pigeons coo, coo
Blackbird incessant
All life seemed, so happy that
Day - not a cry, not a moan
- No 'Do as I say'
            Do you remember

The joy of walking in
Peace together, growing
Children with all their blether,
Smiling, laughing *even* mether
Grannies prattle, Grandad
walking, hell for leather
You do remember!

A Chipperfield

UNTITLED

I gazed at the dragonfly
with sheen on sheer wings -
How does it fly
on such gossamer strings?
How does it hover
sighting its prey,
then off it soars
to hunt far away?
Eyes bulging green
with ferocious glare,
Mouth all a-quiver
it darts through the air.
But now lies quite dead
sucked dry by a foe
Though wings feebly flutter
when gentle winds blow . . .

The sea is full of plastic cups,
That bob at ebb of tide -
Why do we sully sea with such?
Why don't we take more pride?
Why don't we take our rubbish home?
Why dump it in the sea?
'Tis not a local rubbish tip -
'Tis full of life like you and me!

Mia Butler

THE MONOLITHS OF NOWHERE LAND

On windswept wasteland's haunted plains
Where spirit-shadows shift like sand
The concrete ghosts all hand-in-hand
Stand solemn in the evening rain.

And waiting like a shadow-hound
For fox-fur orange lights to die
She crouches under sepia skies
This Supermarket island-town.

Across a car park still as death
Some Coke-cans clenched like hopeless fists
Lie strewn where Love entwined and kissed
In daylight soft as dying breath.

And trolleys waltzing in the wind
Like shrill metallic paramours
Enchained across a moonlit floor
Where sodium lights turn pale and dim.

The distant cries of car alarms
In wailing choirs remote and shrill
Come braying over sunset hills
Across the meads and streams and farms.

These graveyards grey as winter dawns
Where motorways exhale in death
Their roundabouts that curl like breath
Though ozone-Winter's tepid storms.

Julia Wood

SLOTH

Oh Number Seven of Deadly Sins
I know you very well!
Who every mortal battle wins
Will scorn this tale I tell.

That stitch in time I never made
Which could have saved me nine,
I lived to rue, through buttons lost
From clothes, which had been fine.

I didn't make hay while the sun shone,
I was feeling too tired at the time,
Nor did I strike while the iron was hot;
The effort was too sublime.

Yes, I saw those two birds in the bushes,
But my hand was too far away
To stretch right out, so I left them there
To enjoy their innocent play.

I always put off until tomorrow
The things I could do today;
When I shut the gate the horse had gone,
I heard his distant neigh.

I confess I've not even been to the ant
To consider her ways and be wise,
So sluggard I very surely am,
Sluggish beyond surmise.

I've just jumped out of the frying pan
And find myself in the fire;
I opted for the easiest move
Now I fear I shall expire!

Geraldine Squires

PRE-MENSTRUAL TENSION

What is this? Right now it feels like hell,
A violent rage of anger, confusion and feeling unwell.
Yes, that's it, anger at everyone and all,
hang on, though, your control could fall.
I can't, no I want to explode from this shell.

Deep breath, take a deep breath now,
if you don't people will see an absolute cow.
Are you really like that? No, not really,
it's just that my soul is not expressed clearly.
Just wait for it to go, but how? How?

Tension and anger overtake your shattered mind,
inside you feel like being terribly unkind.
You clench your fists wanting to punch something hard,
but really you want to send someone a nice birthday card.
Trying to explain you're Jekyll and Hyde is so very difficult to find.

Are you mad, insane or neurotic, my dear?
No, just a woman with a period near.
A body and soul on the edge of explosion
all because our bodies are full of *oestrogen!*
So if they can't hear too well don't fear.

Why should anyone understand or feel?
only the sufferers know what is real.
So you carry on with your PMT
hoping that people will one day see,
It's not you who is giving off the bad deal

Marie-Louise McCormick

OLD WELLINGBOROUGH

Wellingborough in years gone by,
Was always a happy town.
They didn't have cars all whizzing around.
Only horses and carts could be found.

A trip down the Nene in a rowing boat,
Was quite a familiar sight.
Whilst along its banks was good picnic ground.
You could fish, if you wanted a bite.

The children would play with a large round hoop.
A popular toy in those days.
There was Bassetts Park, or the Castle Fields,
With a bandstand where music was played.

On market day the town was alive,
With stalls set on Market Hill.
A fountain stood proudly among its midst.
To refresh all the travellers at will.

The walks to be sure were a lovely place,
Where people would stroll day by day.
A peaceful and tranquil part of the town,
And this still, can be seen today.

The Sunday school *tea drinking*
A procession, so proudly arrayed.
With everyone dressed in their gay Sunday best.
And they marched while the music was played.

In 1922, a wonderful year,
When the Coronation took place.
Everyone came to the Castle Fields.
To celebrate, all in good taste.

Jill Pettitt

THE TOAD'S ODE

Hello my sweet little damsel fly
Croaked the toad from the bank of his pond
Pray play me a tune on your pan pipes
For us it shall be a new bond

Pretty fly if you like you may call me
I'll play you a tune if you like
But bonds are something quite different
In fact you can get on your bike

Nay sweet little fly do not send me
Away would be too hard to bear
Come pretty do sit beside me
See here I've a nice comfy chair

Comfy chairs are all very well sir
Remember the Princess and frog
I've heard of jewels and furs sir
Next it's *Try a hair of the dog.*

Aye remember the Frog and the princess
How she kissed him full on the lips
How he turned in a trice into something nice
And they both went away on some trips.

J E Hobbs

AWAKENING

That moonlit night was the end of despair.
A glimmer of hope in the vengeful air.
My nightmare ended and my life begun.
Nature my guidance and the moon my sun.
The trees my prison, the moon my soul's light.
At last a breakthrough, the guards lose the fight.
From darkness, depression my heart is free.
My future success I begin to see.

Now two weeks on I'm enlightened, alive.
With new passions, I'll do more than survive.
My direction uncertain, goals unknown.
Nature's my champion, I won't be alone.
The pain of the past has withered and died.
My soul now has meaning where once she cried.
And now I'm happy, with desire again,
The moon on my shoulder warding off bane.

D Black

OPPOSITES

Blue eyes bleed;
Words cannot shout the pain,
But eyes can speak
Shrilly from shattered senses;
Rivers of blood are dammed behind that look,
Where is the storm to break it?

One tongue of lightning
And sparse lips could part,
Screaming their condemnation;
One roll of thunder
And bruised words might start
Growling of dark injustice.

Blue eyes are bleeding,
But no storm has come.

I fix your hurt
And mirror in my look
Your living crucifixion.

Yours is the anger that has fed your pain,
Is mine the balm to break it?

Ruth Sayers

THOUGHTS WHILST WAITING

what will it expel
when my body declares itself ready
when it ejects its contents into the light
its hormonally created load
its chemically based cargo
its predetermined design

my body had the original control
it could have expelled it long ago
but the scales must have balanced
the chances of survival been reasonable

I then took over
my influence brought to bear
to give it a reasonable chance then
that's all.

but what have I put into my body
my body that cannot object
nicotine and alcohol
have I upset that chemical concoction that my body decided safe
have I created a toxic tomb
where limbs and organs and functions will be retarded

it's easy to abuse those you cannot see
to hurt those who cannot answer back
but I may be about to live a life full of guilt
when my body declares itself ready and
ejects its contents into the light.

Sheila Berry

PETER

Peter is divine!
I don't know why I love him so,
It cannot be his mind.

His head is oval,
His nose is big,
His eyes are red or brown,
I love his feet, especially when they're warm,
I love his hair - grey with a touch of brown.

Maybe it's his kindness
or the way he carries himself

There's days I just want to say
'I love you'
But I can't
He just wouldn't understand.

The tables could be turned
It could be him, looking at me, looking at him.

No, he just wouldn't understand.

Because, after all

He's just my *pet rabbit*

Peter!

Karen Rundschke

THE POWER OF LOVE

When I kiss you, I find
Something blows in my mind
And my knees they just want to give way.

The power of your touch
Is sometimes too much
And I find myself feeling afraid.

Scared of what? Do I know?
If I do, should it show?
Well that's up to me to decide.

One thing is for sure
Though I feel insecure
What good does it do if I hide?

My love's so intense
that it doesn't make sense
For me to even try to conceal

The fear deep inside
That *this* won't survive
And that, I'm afraid's very real

It's because it's so good
I've not yet understood
What gives me a right to this *high*

After causing such pain
For my own selfish gain
Who deserves to fall down more than I?

And it's this that I fear
Until you make it clear
That the love you declare is so true

Because if that's so
Then we'll give it a go
And with luck we can surely pull through!

Elaine Stockting

UNTITLED

The morning was bright and sunny,
A gentle breeze refreshed the air
In the village below the mountain
The preacher was saying a prayer.

The women were cooking the dinner
The children were happy in play
The men were doing the odd jobs
But the preacher continued to pray.

At 11-59 on that morning
The mountain suddenly blew its top
Sending the village into panic
But the preacher, he didn't stop.

Lava was thrown down the mountain
Along with hot rocks and ash
The villagers never stood a chance
Their homes were gone in a flash.

The smell of the refreshing air
Replaced by acrid poisonous gas
Nothing was left of the village
Not a tree nor blade of grass.

Only one body was ever recovered
From that now forgotten land
Preserved in the silt from the landslide
The preacher with prayer book in hand.

Nick Green

IT

To the children it's a place to wash and play.
To clean away the dirt and grime of the day.
To dad it's a den, he locks the door,
To read and smoke for almost an hour.
To me it's a haven of peace and tranquillity
To lose myself, and escape completely.
This place must be important, it has letters you see,
So what's this grand place?
Why the WC.

Fiona Woodward

BEING BIG

Being big is not a crime
Our feelings do get hurt sometimes
It may not show, but it is true
For we are human just like you.
Hearing quips silly rhymes
I've heard them all a thousand times
Each time I laugh and hide the pain
Knowing it will come again
When you say fat jokingly
It's a laugh for you but not for me
So think before you speak please do
I could have easily been you.

J Kennedy

IN THE CITY

The streets are not all paved with gold,
but with dirt and grime and litter;
and cardboard cities decry from the corners
with people forlorn and lost and bitter . . .
in the city.

There's money being spent by County Hall,
renovations to give the city a new look;
lest we forget those who have suffered,
the children of the city whose lives they took . . .
in the city.

The grey of its towers strut above the skyline
now, facade of mustiness, hangs, like a cloud;
The streets milling with the shopping people,
people who were once, so proud . . .
of the city.

Exhaust fumes from the motor vehicles,
and plumes of toxins rising up from chimneys
all add to the contractual destruction
that's bringing the town to its knees . . .
in this, our city.

And how can we, as ordinary people put right the wrong
that has been done to the heritage, to architectural beauty
once heralded as the dreaming spires
but now surely becoming, a dying, and poor city . . .

our world, our lives are all . . .
in the city.

Ron Matthews Jr

FRONDESCENCE

You feel the frost, and in your eyes
I see the colours turn,
The foliage deep within you lies;
The golds and russets burn.

Once as a gatepost, there I stood
Within your meadows' bound,
We co-existed - woods and wood
Yet shared no common ground.

I watched the seasons, from my spot
Transform your fertile trees,
As I endured decay and rot
Against the stinging breeze.

And then one day, a flower bloomed
From out my splintered side,
Above my head your birches loomed
As if with curious pride.

So now fall's harvest rules us both,
The field is overgrown,
The soil remembers summer's growth
And thanks the seeds we've sown.

Tom Bartlett

THE SOLITARY EVENING PRIMROSE

The evening light slowly fades away,
At the end of a warm summer's day;
All things put on their night attire,
And to their weary dreams retire.

But one extends the daylight hour,
By lighting up her lantern tower;
Helping the friendly sight to stay,
While shadowy bats wait to play.

Everything shortly will be locked and gone,
After the evening's watering has been done;
Only then is left the prayer and care,
Of the garden's tall lady with the lamp.

She will watch through the uncertain night,
But the flame will go out when tomorrow is bright;
It will be re-kindled for the following dark,
To continue the self-effacing work.

E Ashwell

THOUGHTS ON AUTUMN

Soft mists of autumn rolling over the hills -
A wind from the sea blowing cold.
Blackberries hide beneath the hedge
And millions of leaves turn gold.

Toadstools and mushrooms grow in the grass
And spider webs glow in the dew.
Squirrels and weasels are hunting for food
But the nuts on the ground are few.

Wild swans in the sky have come from the cold -
But the swallows have flown to the warm.
The first trace of frost is on the pond
And the field-mice hide in the corn.

When all the crops are gathered in,
It's harvest festival time.
We can all give thanks for the food that has grown
And the beauty of autumn time.

Rosemary Babbington

NURSE

You call
and as I turn to see
You twist and call to someone else
Someone loved
but dead.
My caring capabilities have to stop there
I cannot pretend they are here,
I'm twisting
Spiralling in my own unique confusion,
I cannot ask someone else to help
For they may tell you what you don't want to know.
If you're told they're dead,
It would be for the first time
Your misery would erupt.
So we pretend,
Again.

Louise Christopher

WHAT IS POETRY?

Poetry is the linguist's playground.
When a phrase encapsulates the strength and subtlety of mankind's most powerful emotions.
When words slot into place like the pieces of a well-made jigsaw,
Or slide off the honeyed tongue like the smooth silken stroke of a lover's caress,
Or flit and tumble onto the page like a rabble of disorderly butterflies.

Catriona Mackay

WALK RIGHT IN

He walked up to me
And looked
His eyes into mine
He was beautiful
Blonde on blonde
He spoke
What did he say
Did he speak
My glass was empty
I wanted another Gin
So many people
So hot
My eyes rose from the glass
His eyes still looking for an answer
The answer was in my eyes

R G Jones

THE LAZY HOUSEWIFE

I'm sitting in the armchair, the sun is streaming in,
I haven't done the washing and the kids are making a din.
I'm curled up nice and small and, the sun shows all the dirt,
That's all along the window ledge, still I guess it doesn't hurt.
My old man won't be back, well not for two days maybe more,
He's gone on a business trip, I'm lonely what a bore.
So, I'll clean the house right through and I'll do the washing up,
I'll play with the kids and maybe cook a dish with duck.
I'll brush the dog, I'll sweep the floor and maybe given time,
I'll even visit Mother and other relatives of mine.
But, my armchair is rather comfy and the sun is nice and warm,
and the kids will be quite happy if they play out on the lawn,
Fish and chips will do for diner and there's lemonade to drink,
In fact I'm fairly organised so I'll just have 40 winks.

Amanda L Clarke

A VICTIM'S PLEA

How do I feel,
You look so wan
How do I feel
As he lets me carry the can.

I feel like a fragile piece of glass
Shattered into a million fragments,
like a zombie awakened from the dead
Seeing in each new day filled with dread
My heart is in my stomach
My mind is filled with guilt
Why did I let it happen
It's with me all the time.

I begged, I *pleaded* all in vain
He still hurt me, be in pain, again
and again.
Why do they do it, they are rotten to the core,
Hate fills my very being,
It comes out of every pore.

Now a few months later,
I feel I've been reborn,
To live in this lonely land,
To see in each new morn.

My spirit's getting stronger now
I won't let him win
I've stopped him for now
I just hope that they won't let
him out, to commit another sin
and put some other girl
through the *hell* where I've been.

Sara Stredwick

I WONDER . . .

. . . And as I sit upon some hill
To ponder life, when all is still,
Is there, on some other plane
A man and mountain just the same?
And does he sit and contemplate
The whys and wherefores of *his* fate?
And do his musings make him cry
Or can he see beyond the sky?
Might he be privy to some plot
And knows of plans that we do not . . .?
Is his spirit wise, aware
Of hidden secrets way out there?
Is there some unknown energy,
Some force, some electricity -
Undetected by our senses,
Ridiculing our pretences . . .?
And is space empty - just a void?
Or is it secretly employed,
Invisible; no sight, no sound
Betrays it to us earthly-bound?

And when I die and leave this sphere,
This *spark* that's me might still be here -
And if there is another place
Then will I find your smiling face . . .?
Or do we, buried and forgot,
Return into a melting pot . . .?

I do hope not!

Lesley Janet Green

THE GARDEN

I sat in the garden one evening,
The sun was shining bright.
The sound of the blackbirds singing, the trees
were a beautiful sight.
Their leaves as green as emeralds, were swaying
in the breeze.
The Garden is a lovely place, to sit and take
your ease, but as the sun went down
at night, the clouds began to form.
Big ones - black ones, and then a
thunder storm.

L M Nickels

OUR FAMILY TREE

(Dedicated to my parents Alfred and Dorothy Riley)

You were the roots to anchor us all.
And the trunk, so strong straight and tall.
The wood inside so good and true,
We are the boughs that branched out of you,
The leaves your crowning glory,
Your children and grandchildren.
Each year more leaves grow, and so it goes on
Each one a part of you.
But now you have gone, chopped down before your
prime.
An empty space left, where once you stood,
Your branches and leaves spread far and wide.

But wait, some seedlings are sprouting,
Your great-grandchildren
A new generation, and a new life
All from you,
The strong root stock.

Patricia M Freeman

A QUESTION OF FAITH

When I lay beneath the velvet sky
and gaze at the stars in the milky way;
When darkness surrounds me like a cloak
and the moon shines down with her silver ray;
When the vastness of space and the galaxies whirl
and the planetary systems their glories unfurl,
then into my mind come the questions of life -
does this really derive from an almighty bang
or do I detect a Creator's hand?

When the waters ripple and reflections stir
as I sit by the lake in the heat of the day;
When the leaves dance in the gentle breeze
as I watch the ducklings and cygnets at play;

When the kingfisher swoops and the silver fish hides
and the arctic tern circles and hovers and dives,
then the questions of life come into my mind -
Can we really believe life evolved from a blob?
It takes much less faith to believe in a God.

Did man really come from the ape and its kind?
Did we gain by accident our incredible mind
that can grapple with thoughts, with love, with hate,
that can solve our problems, alter our fate?
No!
I believe that the wonder of man,
of this beautiful world and creation, can
only be part of a master plan.
It was made for us by a God who cares,
who loves us all and with whom He shares
his life, which He gave for all mankind,
that forgiveness and freedom in Him we can find.

Mary Garbutt

THE SHOEMAKER'S LAMENT

Cross-legged on the ground he sits
A shoe between his knees
With awl, *thread,* and a block of wax
The tacks between his teeth
No machine in all the world, could ever be as neat
As shoehand Jack with his craftsman's eye
And his regular even stitch
For a pair of shoes that are made by hand
Are a joy to behold and wear
But alas, these days they are things of the past
And rarely ever seen.
The uppers were made from the finest calf
Then moulded to fit the feet
Lucky are those who can boast a pair
Of hand made leather shoes.
Now in this modern plastic age
Footwear monstrosities have taken their place
Pouring off the assembly lines
At an incredible speed, boxed and labelled
Dispatched with haste
All ready for the nation's feet
And soon *'my duck'* when we hobble along
Between a couple of sticks, carpet slippered, and surgical boots
With a chit for the chiropodist
A nation of cripples we shall be
Unless we recapture the past,
Returning to the days of yore.
When shoes were made to last.

George Kitchen

SUNSET MEMORIES

With wide arms outstretched and
Beckoning comfort to my aching back
You - are always there
Faded - weary and worn - with patches, bare
Yet, you, are always there
Family and friends have had their entrances and exits
You, welcomed and comforted all - because
You, were always there
My old and favourite chair

We have aged together, you and I
At the end of the day
We will say good-bye
Someone will take you, I don't know where
My old and favourite chair.

Joan Staniforth

LOVE

Nature has her own devices
For changing virtues into vices.
Is loving deeply but a sin
An endless battle none can win?

No reasoned words can curb emotion
No reasoned words can stop devotion
No reasoned words will ever chide
Such heartfelt love so deep inside.

Love knows no barrier, has no shame
Defies convention, plays no game
No reasoned words will ever dim
The constant flame that burns within . . .

Brian A Morris

UNTITLED

All the treasures of the world are mine
The secret of this joy divine
Lies in the beauty of your eyes
The warm deep timbre of your voice
The intricacies of your desires.
Moods - fleeting as the sun and wind
Borne on a flirty April morn

Strength: in your hands, gentle and fine, your arms of steel
Your body, hard, so hard for me, yet in the answer to my plea
A soft luxurious resting place

Oh! I am dizzy with this wine, intoxicated with fire and heat
Brought to me by this wine so sweet, which stems from love
Brings ecstasy from this cup of life, this cup of life is you.

You entrance me, taunt me with your whims, with your exquisite torments
You will ever hold my thirsty heart without a need of chains or vice
Yet, as two lonely songbirds skim, so swift - oh heaven sent!
Across the morning air, so far apart are you and I.
But it is somehow wise to secrete a precious thought
Retain an atom of individuality, whilst giving all,
Whilst being one

Oh this, a dream of paradise as thick as honey, clear as ice
Each feeling one which penetrates, all life, all death
No compromise, no shadows, all awareness, sweet perception
Piercing, singing, shouting, sobbing, all emotions felt unto their limit
We are the sun, the universe, so great, magnificent
A golden burst of glory, molten, showering the mundane earth with living joy

And now, green, cool, so dark, a scented gloom, deep, ever deep
A peace before unknown to man, in this forever will we sleep.

Janice Hunter

WORLD'S CONTENT

So many people have lost their way
Embarrassment and fear is what they say
Listen and learn to things all around you
Take notes, live life you know it's true.

Hungry people living on the streets
People dying left unfound for weeks
Children crying having no parents to care
Wars that mean nothing, just stripping life bare.

Is this the world in which we choose to live?
Or do we change, instead of take, we give.
How long will it be before everything goes
Can you ignore what's in front of your nose?

Merry Christmas everybody, that's what we say
But it's back to the rat-race the very next day
Why do we celebrate when we don't really believe?
Our world is full of hypocrisy, pain and greed.

So many people with no one to love
Tomorrow bringing someone that fits like a glove
Their hearts cry out for expression and feeling
Too many broken hearts, you're out of the dealing.

Death comes to many as a long cherished dream
Slowly but surely too tired even to scream
The pain will go, the suffering complete
It's the ones who are left who need to find their feet.

Lesley Pszkit

THINK FIRST

Don't once support because it's a trend.
Don't follow the crowd to popular be:
For a raving crowd could a victim's life end:
Late penalty judge popularity.

Don't follow a trend by lack of thought.
Don't run like frightened sheep away.
Only by *considered reasons* support.
Be sure it's worthwhile; a justified way.

How foolish it is to be swept with the tide
Of a trend or present popular sway.
Unthinking persons no depth to bide
When going gets tough along the way.

Consider therefore before you support,
What value or trend or fashion be.
Think for yourself, and decide as you ought,
'Is it really worthwhile for others or me?'

So give good reasons to really support
That you're not just like 'fair-weather' friend.
If you campaign, it needs careful thought
So it's worthwhile to be loyal to the end.

William Holland

THE MOON

Like an eye in the night,
Glowing faintly in the morning light.
Remember it'll always be there,
As if hanging in mid-air.
Waiting for the cold to pass away.
Waiting to round up another summer's day.

Like an opening to the heavens above,
Shining like a white dove.
Playing hide and seek with the clouds.
Whispers heard amongst nature's sounds.
Mystical dreams never gone too soon.
Magical fantasies dreamt under the moon.

Shahnaz Choudhury

SHORT TENNIS

He talks like a deaf child
all his vowels are open
the edges curl away from him
he listens with a half-inverted gaze,
selects a service break at which he intervenes.
He profits from it
as we profit from a timely change in channel,
a shuffle round the upper deck.
It's where we meet him sociable and absent
his ease is palpable,
his hazard negligible,
ever in our debt yet we are the more indebted.
we offer him an opening
smooth the table clear for demonstration,
lighted up like Abelard we Heloise him,
His tone is wider than is wanted,
we are too small for him,
we feel our lack.
It shames us that we adhere to substance
when form is far the best mode of attack.

Rose Croghan

FREE AS AN EAGLE

The eagle has its domain
Nobody there to complain
Free up there in the sky
Oh! I wish I could fly
The freedom must be bliss
With only the wind to kiss
The air so clean and pure
That is for sure
Solitude away from things
Going round the air in rings
Up and down
No need to frown
Wings I wish I had too
To join that eagle in the sky so blue.

Malcolm W Davison

A DILEMMA

Do you lie or tell the truth?
With neither do you gain
But love, respect and trust becomes
Just bitterness and pain.

Even little fibs, like ivy grow
Such seemingly pretty leaves
And this complex web can to concrete cling
As the deception climbs and weaves

Until the root is weeded out
And the secrets finally die.
With past happiness and truth
Devoured by one white lie.

Vivien Mary Phillips

MOTHER LOVES YOU, WHEREVER YOU ARE
(A CHILD'S FUNERAL)

The sight so bright, the joy of flowers amongst the murmerous, heedless bees.
A garden? No!
These blooms will never come to seed.
No fruit will fall to fertile ground, their children lost to us.
No rose to scent the air as this one does - cut down before its life was done.
A sweet revenge to please our sense? No!
A token of love for all to share, an expression of grief for one so fair.
A flood of colour at our feet, a blanket of beauty for a winding sheet.

My Love, my Child will never rise to grace the day with dewy eyes.
Cut down like the rose is Heaven's prize.
Gone are the hands so soft and sweet - the noisy ever-running feet.
I'll never hear him laugh again, or cover him against the rain.
Oh! Does he cry for me somewhere?
Oh God! I wish that I were there to wipe away each shining tear.
Dear Lord, please keep him in Your Care!

Gill Lyden

IMPOSSIBLE DREAMS

Oh how I wish that I could stand
Or run along a golden strand,
And watch the foaming waves break up upon the shore
Would any normal person ask for more?
Or maybe just to climb a long steep hill?
And there another wish I would fulfil,
To stand and gaze upon the view spread out below.
Just to do, no limits to, where anyone can go,
But mortal bonds, that hold so strong, make desires be confined
To wishful thoughts and hopeless dreams, imprisoned in my mind,
For my role's been cast, my part set fast
A paraplegic to the last.

S Doran

LOST YET AGAIN

A tender face held by a fragile hand,
a climbing rose, a deserted land,
a fallen star, a disconcerting light,
Come . . . climb into my heart at night.

Without an intrepid glance,
or a lifetime filled with haste,
Come . . . my honey dew-dappled skin will glisten,
do you dare to taste?

Outstretched fingers grapple for a little time,
legs entangled, writhing, mad,
how far can you reach as you climb and climb?

Was it a day or was it a year?
Was that droplet of sweat really a tear?

Keep climbing, don't stop!

A frenzied flame faltering in the shadows,
an explosion of fire, a half-eaten rose,
bruise my lips with your words before you go,
in a haze iridescent with gold and indigo.

Natasha Wright

OXFORD

Oxford the city of inspiration and dreams
Where people can study and achieve high esteem,
With beautiful buildings of ancient design
Now crowded by misfits of seventies clime,
Where grammar and English make a last stand
With visitors bemused by its strange local brand
From over the world tourists come from afar
And young ones seek action in nightclub and bar.

Its history living through brand name and commerce
Rover, Frankcooper, Fleming, and Alice
Blackwell founder of library now famous for books,
Its parks and museums all well worth a look
Of punting and rivers and Magdalen Bridge
Surrounded by country, and white horse ridge.
Oxford a city of diversement abound
A magical mix of town and of gown

Jane Darnell

THE QUALITY OF LIFE

What is, 'the quality of life'? - What do we mean?
Unsolved mysteries of illness defy medical knowledge
Thousands die of starvation
Crops fail - pestilence prevails
What is the quality of life?
Hostages are taken - terrorists are shot
Is the power of life greater than the quality?
Foetus's are aborted day after day
What price life?
Wars are rife the world over
Nation against nation
Culture against culture
Religion against religion.
What happened to tolerance
And brotherly understanding?
Unemployment breeds boredom,
Boredom breeds violence,
Violence breeds death.
What happened to life and living?
What and where is 'the quality of life'?

Adam Brent

POOR OLD DAD

To the pushers of today
Youth are easy prey

They turn brother against brother
His father and his mother

The methods are uncouth
They batten onto youth

They say everything's for you
But if they only knew

They mean we want your money
So come on sonny

They say don't listen to your dad
He's too old

We know best just do as your
Told

They supply the drugs to all
The young mugs

They sell them the dope and
The slippery slope

The money down the drain
The damage to the brain

The life of despair with
Eyes that only stare

Yes they do show the way to
The unsuspecting stray

But poor old dad he's too old
He knows nothing they are told

So who do we blame, 'TV' movies
Or schools?

For the plight of these poor
Young fools

No matter who we blame the
Picture is still the same

Drug taking gets worse,
Taking drugs is bad

With little joy if any
For poor old dad

Maurice Shea

UNTITLED

In the still of the night, I whisper your name,
Nothing to me will ever seem the same.
The moment you went, I stopped living too,
I am still so much in love with you.

In the still of the night, I tell you my dreams,
What I have done, and how the days seem
Without you beside me to show me the way.
Memories of you are here to stay.

In the still of the night, I remember through the tears
Of us being together, being happy through the years
Longing for our cuddles and kisses too
Never in this world can there be another you.

In the still of the night, I gaze at your photo so dear
This is the time when I feel you so very near,
I look at your dear face and whisper goodnight,
See you in the morning my darling, sleep tight.

M E Constant

GRANDMA'S DELIGHT

Our Sal is expecting a baby!
Now what do you think to that?
I knew she was keeping a secret
She's been just like an old Cheshire cat.

Perhaps I could tell old Gertie next door
I know she's kept all my secrets before,
But what do I care if the whole world knows
That we'll soon have a grandchild twiddling its toes?

Tomorrow I'll fly down the shops for some wool,
They'll soon know what's happened when my basket is full
Of ribbons and laces and patterns galore,
But I just can't keep it to myself any more.

Oh, oh, oh, I'm thrilled to the marrow
I'm dancing about with joy,
I'm hopping about like a sparrow
Thank You God for this bundle of joy.

Ida Wootton

THOUGHTS ON YOUR SILVER WEDDING

You have come through joy, laughter, sadness and all the tears.
The sun shining through the clouds of grey with the passing years
The road through life is never smooth but you never lost the way
Together you have walked side by side to this special day.
I wish you both the very best as memories today unfold.
And after your Silver Wedding Day look forward to the
Gold.

Sheila Lane

A HUNTER'S DYING RACE

Hooligans of sick intent
Until their violence is spent
Have no regard for kith or kin
To 'murder' they regard no sin.

Or do they 'hide' from their abuse?
If questioned, they have no excuse;
They dress the *same* for all to see
Their *shame* in anonymity.

They've horses 'high', but low esteem,
For fewer want to join their team.
'Out our way!' - They thunder past.
. . . 'Gentle-men? Where is your class?'

No dignity you can portray;
Savage thugs in disarray.
Give up *now*. Admit defeat!
- You're fast becoming obsolete.

Ann James

MY DIET

Some diets are fast and some are slow
Those extra pounds really must go
Measure this and measure that
To start with you feel such a prat
As weeks go past you can predict
I have become a diet addict
Twenty pounds I lost today
Right let's have a Chinese Take-away.

Paul Miller

SILENT PRAYER

Take a look inside my head,
And tell me what you see.
Dust aside the tangled webs,
And set my thinking free.
Watch my thoughts spill and flow,
In whirlpools spinning round,
They never know which way to go,
They tumble to the ground.
Take the pain and watch it squirm,
Squash it until it dies.
Smile at the love, and she will learn
To soothe the hidden cries.
See the anger, unlock his key,
And let the wrath burn out,
Take the hurt and set it free,
Then watch it fade to naught.
Kindle the joy until she glows,
And unveil the gentle soul,
Then, close the door and softly go,
And know you've made me whole.

Diana Bending

A LONELY DREAM

I was standing in a lonely place,
a place full of quiet and fear,
my heart began to race,
with the oncoming steps I hear.

The footsteps stop and shuffle,
as if in deep meditation,
my breathing I try to muffle,
I long to run with no retaliation.

In the distance I could hear,
a sound so loud and hoarse,
I still kept quiet but with fear,
but I cannot change my course.

All of a sudden there was light,
no one was there, it would seem,
even when quiet and fear was my plight
I knew that it was all but a dream.

T Austin

MARRIAGE

Our wedding day
Young, in love
Two hearts, joined as one
We were not prepared for what lay ahead!
Nobody told us it was a hard road to tread.
Lack of understanding
Poor communication
Two hearts, torn apart
When did it all start to go wrong?
The togetherness we had has all gone.
Hurts, open wounds
We are both in pain.
Forgiveness, healing
We are in love again.
An act of will
Determination
God inspired
Gift of marriage.

C A Pattinson

SONNET TO THE NHS

It has not been my year of that I am sure.
When I broke my left wrist I didn't want more

But I broke it again falling off a steep kerb
Damaged my back - more than I deserved

Then my eyesight grew worse and became very bad
Two cataracts clouded my vision - how sad!

After that I couldn't put heel to the floor
Till cortisone made me able to go to the door.

But what I will say is 'Well done, NHS.'
Who treated me royally in all my distress.

The wrist neatly plastered, quite easy to bear;
My backside was treated with physio's care

Cataracts replaced by implants quite brilliant
Go NHS! You too'll be resilient.

Dolly Harmer

THE ANT

Why do you so hard strive
To keep your fellow workers alive
Is it from some fraternal love
That in man would be duly ordained from above
Or that it is which we have to accept
A form of duty we would not expect
But to live a life in earnest endeavour
And no cross words between each ever
It is something beyond our thought
Or ethics in social science taught.

Brian Norman

HER ROOM

The maiden's room looks East
Across the silken sea into the face of dawn.
The sun kisses bougainvillaea and white walls
Shattering the mist-glow into promise,
Promise of day, promise of light and love.
She smiles in hope.

The mother's room looks South.
The sun is high and hot.
She shades her children from the glare of life
And seeks herself the shadow of their love.
That love is there, and joy is there.
She smiles, fulfilled.

The widow's room looks West.
The heat of day is gone. Her man has gone.
The sunset burns with tired gleam.
No children call. She sits alone.
The evening drops its cloak across the sea.
She smiles in memory.

The greyhead's room looks North.
The sun has gone for ever. Life is cold.
Weary, she nods all day and longs for darkness.
Only the night remains
And sleep, quiet sleep.
She smiles in hope.

Stephen Holley

LOVE YOU FOREVER

I will love you forever even after I've gone
For a love so so deep cannot be left forlorn

I will treasure the places we went to together
The laughter and tears we shared unashamedly

The time has now come for me to go to
The Good Lord in Heaven as He told me to do

Still we'll visit the places we went to together
When you'll feel a soft breeze you'll know I am there

Don't be gloomy and sad in your days 'cause I've gone
Your just whisper my name and I'll be with you anon

Right there by your side to protect you from harm
I will always be there if you just hold my hand

You're my angel on earth you're my star you're my sun
I will love you forever even more now I've gone

Iride Helena Cerbelli

A GOOD MOTHER

A good mother's a wonderful blessing,
A blessing from Heaven above,
She'll help you in all times of trouble,
And shower you daily with love.

She'll often give things to her children,
That she really could do with herself,
And if needs be, she'll work to support them,
Even when in a poor state of health.

But often her deeds are forgotten,
By many who leave her warm nest,
And when she's too old to look after herself,
To them she's an unwelcome guest.

But a few remember their mother,
Their blessing from Heaven above,
And in her time of need they will help her,
And shower her daily with love.

Nicola Coleman

MARRIED BLISS

Do this, don't do that
Wipe your feet upon the mat.

Straighten your tie, hang up your hat
Put out that light, put out the cat.

Up in the morning, first out of bed
Unkind thoughts are best left unsaid.

Give me the toothpaste, put on the cap
Shut the door, turn off the tap.

Don't burn the toast, pour out the tea
Put down that paper and look at me.

Come help get the kids to school
Don't stand there gaping like a fool.

Put on your coat, go catch your train
Don't dare use that bad word again.

What can we do to put things right
Come, give me a kiss, my heart's delight.

Yvonne-Marie Payne

A LONELY FEAR

What is it to be all alone,
Sitting in silence in an empty home,
It's worse at night when you're getting sleepy,
Every little thing seems really creepy,
You turn your head and see shadows of the night,
Your heart skips a beat and gives you a fright,
Each little sound sends your imagination wild,
You feel as insecure as a four year old child,
You want somebody there to make you feel alright,
The really spooky thing is the absence of the light,
All strange thoughts go racing through your brain,
The loneliness you feel inside is a dull aching pain,
Eventually you fall asleep and explore all the dreams
you find,
That is until you're jolted awake by your subconscious
mind.

Claire Stevenson

A HEDGEHOG'S FAREWELL

For our comrade lying here
Pause an instant, shed a tear
He lodges now in hedgehog heaven
For trying to cross the A127

We gather round him in our grief
His time amongst us just too brief
He stood four square for things of matter
But now, alas, he's mostly flatter

Let his sobbing widow (on the left)
And pretty youngsters, now bereft
Take these words and be inspired
He hasn't gone. he's just re-tyred.

Ol' Slimjim

AUTUMN

No breeze was felt,
Or seen to move,
And yet -
Gently falling -
To the ground,
A solitary leaf.

The golden leaf,
So bright to see,
Its life -
Now at an end.
Had fallen -
From its home above,
With slow serenity.

No reason was there,
To be seen -
Why this small leaf,
Should fall,
But very soon its -
Friends above were,
Answering the call.

A gentle shower,
Of falling leaves.
Covering all below,
Our single leaf,
Hidden now,
Beneath the -
Carpet of the woods.

Roy Turland

THE LAST DAY OF MY WORLD

The first dawn of a new world breaks through the darkness
Mist from the sea draws in, air so moist and fresh, the softness of my skin
Breeze that blows the waves across the sea
The smell that fills my soul, so free so fresh in my thoughts
Whispers that rush through my hair, the pain it blows away
Though a shadow of disbelief may threaten me
Life was hard, worth living even suffering
Seagulls overhead, a thousand voices raised together in song
Single and solitary the bird that flies above the sun
The sky begins to darken
Jet black and colourless, but so full of warmth and life
Sparkling lights so bright and tiny in the sky
As the moon casts its face upon this earth for the last night

Sandra Norris

TWO O'CLOCK IN THE MORNING BLUES

Gath'ring the air into a warm embrace
I find cold comfort in the empty space,
and the only answer to a silent cry
is the quieter minute as it passes by
that pauses to place a gentle kiss
to remind me of the hour and the man I miss.
But you can't hold them back - the tears or the man -
so I let them go free and forget if I can
Oh, but I keep my fist tight, though I'm still going to lose
these hours meant for sleep in exchange for the blues.

Rachael Catt

DAY DREAMS

Misshapen happiness in terms of dreams,
Comes overnight when darkness seams
Walls and sockets, light and haze,
Gone are the long, day dreamy days.

Effortless moments and empty meanders,
Trip from the tongue like endless candours;
Picture book laughter and daisy fields,
These the day no longer yields.

Dull sodden thoughts, strung with mute wonders,
Through dawn to dusk with countless blunders,
Arrive uninvited with strict notes,
Into the room, where he now dotes.

Smiling in wonder at stupid mistakes,
Waiting for love that surely makes
Him happy again, and smiles once more
Slide from the sky, through bolted door.

P Bullock

THOUGHTS

When I perceive the perfect day.
I think of you so far away.
Of things we did when we were young
The games we played beneath the sun
Oh happy days so long ago
Did we ever really know
That life is fleeting, soon gone by.
As winking as the starry sky
I often wonder now I'm old
If there's a moment we could hold
We both would choose the self-same one
That Perfect day of golden sun.

June Clare

MY LOVER

Soft as a touch of misty dreams
Your lips meet mine, my heart takes flight,
I tremble on the brink of dreams
Dare I proceed? It feels so right.

Your warm kind eyes and face so true
Beguile me to believe it's right.
This precious love I feel for you
Perhaps one day you will requite.

I stand in awe - your smiles entice.
Your touch thrills tremors in my heart.
Is this all real? This Paradise
Please stay my love, do not depart.

Twice-fold the pains and all the tears
Our life's long journey filled with stress.
But loving arms can calm our fears
And soothe us with a sweet caress.

My love is free without a tie.
It's yours to take or throw away.
It is my privilege to try
To dispel your pains of yesterday.

I sometimes feel when we're apart.
My dreams must be a fallacy.
But when you hold me to your heart
You take me through to ecstasy.

If a thousand dreams could culminate
And I could catch them from above,
I'd let them all participate
And look at you - and see my love.

Sylvia Johnson

OUR HOUSE MARTINS

In velvety *coats,*
No feathers forlorn,
They arrive, to put others to scorn,
Their flight, unsurpassed,
As they skim the ground,
Their skills at diving,
And screaming abuse,
Feeding on the wing,
On anything that is found, and,
That flies on the wind.
No escape from these
Pirates of the breeze,
That feed, as fast as the blink of an eye
Their nests are such, that hang from walls
Or under roofs, of cottage thatch.
The brood is not very long
In coming to the hatch,
And, with mouths agape,
They scream, for food.
Which parents, unerringly find,
And fly at speed, and brake,
In an instant of time.
To fill, the waiting mouths,
Then away, to scream again.
These noisy sirens of the skies,
Always, make us think in the main,
That summer, is here, once again.

R Gordon Tilley

MY WINTER DREAM

The scene, is simply magical;
When the snow is all around:
Like a brand new, pastel carpet,
lying neatly, on the ground.

The footprints there; are many:
but they have a part, to play;
with their varied, shapely patterns;
in the carpet, every day.

The highway; draws attention;
for there's snow, slush, either side.
It makes the stretch, seem narrow;
when in fact, it's rather wide.

The snow clad trees, are magical;
in the winter morning light;
and they still retain their impact;
when observed, at fall of night.

The fields are almost, hidden,
by the avalanche of snow;
and the birds, leave tiny imprints;
as up, and down, they go.

Inspiration, builds intensely,
as I catch the falling snow;
and as it clouds my Vision;
the words, just overflow!

I stay; in the blinding snowstorm;
to continue, my winter dream
For my world of words, is uppermost:
Simply Magical; is the theme:

Patricia-Mary Gross

WITCH HUNT OF AN INNOCENT

She stands alone against the sky
And gazes at the starry night
Asking of the heavens - why -
The sleeping world ignores her plight.

'Where lies the curséd spells in these?'
She asks - 'in marigold, in this wild thyme?
What evil lurks in these bay leaves,
And conjures up such wicked crime?'

'Here lies my trade - to ease the pain
Of life - from tender plants of earth -
To kill this ageing woman is insane -
They are but fools - were fools at birth.

'They must know that I have done no harm,
for persecution, in this way -
But, here 'tis written, in my palm
That in my fate I have no say'

Linda Hardy

FOR MY MUM

Whenever you are near,
The feeling is very clear,
Our love will last for ever.
The days we spend, the clothes you lend,
The memories of you are treasured.

Though parted we are . . . the distance is far . . .
I'll always be near,
The vision is clear . . .
These memories will last forever.

Lindsay Ephgrave

TO A LOST LOVE

Why can't I make your feelings fair,
Flick a switch and they'll be there,
Just, toss a coin and turn it round,
Roll over a stone and it will be found,
Deal straight aces from the deck,
Pour in concrete, make it set,
Sweep away, the dying cinders,
Light a fire, that forever lingers,
Push back the clouds that darken the day
Shove! That void away,
Just to hold your hand once more, without
being shown the door,
To make you happy, instead of sad,
To make you a prince, instead of a Cad.
To make you listen, instead of shout,
To give me love, with nothing taken out,
To hold a light, that never dies,
To never listen, to endless lies,
To start, all over again,
Without the pain.

M O'Connell-Almond

THE NIGHT WIND

Listen to its howling its moans and groans,
Listen to its anger tearing down homes,
Gathering speed up hill and down dale,
Hark at young babies beginning to wail!

Rushing through forests wailing and sighing,
Creaking through homes . . . slumber denying,
Fences breaking, gates banging, chimney-pots flying, garage
doors slamming,

Trees swaying in spite of their might,
The great wind commands it . . . King of the night!

But slowly, slowly, as if tiring of fun,
Its howls and its moans become merely a hum,
The night once more sleeps . . .
And only a whisper can be heard through dark alleys and
long narrow streets.

Annette Showler

SCANDAL

Someone could have told me sooner
That they'd heard another rumour
Then at least I'd have a chance to put a stop -
To not just that, but all the others,
That I've heard about the lovers,
The lovers that I didn't know I'd got!

You see the funny thing with gossip
Is that when you think you've lost it
It just creeps up right behind you once again,
And I guess it's kind of sad
When it's making someone glad,
If their heart turned into weather it would rain -

- Snuffing out somebody's candle,
Causing yet another scandal
To widen a few spaces between friends,
Lots of tears and lots of pain
To drag through someone's name,
The truth need not be broken when it bends.

Jonathan Spencer

WISHING

I wish the world a better place
Nobody hungry
Nobody poor
Dame Fortune knocking at the door
No more suffering
No more pain
And all over the world no war
Enemies and friends shaking hands
Even in the foreign lands
No colour bar
Or race relations
No fighting or killing
Between the nations
I know it's a dream
But it could be true
How about starting
With me and you.

S Hickman

REVOLUTION

All hope is gone, it did not occur,
The miracle I seek.
I feel tossed, by the storm, and emotional
and weak.
But the stars still glow,
And the sun still shines,
The world still turns around.
If the grass is green and the flowers grow,
Then joyfulness is found.

Jean Hatton

THUNDERSTORM
(For Gillian Tillman)

With bated breath it seems
All nature waits,
Until in blinding
Blue-white light
The night
Evaporates.

Hear rain invisible
Clattering through
The agitated
Squall-swept trees
Whose leaves
Beat the tattoo.

The lightning forks to earth
Dazzling the eye,
And by the sudden
Crackling powers
See flowers
Flash-bloom and die.

The drumming thunder rolls
Further away;
Amid flying clouds
Stars appear,
So clear
Before the day.

Jim Finch

PLAYING WITH THE CAT

So I'm sitting in my thinking room
t'was peaceful, quiet, but then
I heard a little scratching noise,
that crazy Cat again

I tore a sheet of *Andrex* off
and poked it 'neath the door,
I knew what was expected
having played this game before.

Like Henry Cooper's uppercut
a slash of unseen paw
ripped half the sheet of paper off
with razor sharpened claw

First round to the Pussy Cat,
I tore another sheet,
of late, my furry little friend
was getting hard to beat

My second piece of toilet roll
just vanished without trace.
I must admit, a big broad grin
had spread across my face

That pesky Cat was getting good,
too good for me by half,
so when the third sheet disappeared
I really had to laugh

Then I heard a little chuckle
and I knew that I'd been had
when a girl's voice laced with laughter said
'You're really stupid, Dad.'

Bruce Harvey

OCTOBER

The dark days of winter are drawing near
Alas! the summer's gone, I fear
No more the sky, is bright and blue
The World takes on, a different hue
The leaves of green, turn to gold and brown,
And blustery winds, send them hurtling down
Trees are blown down, window panes rattle
Sheep huddle together for warmth
As gale force winds, across the fields do blow.
Fields that in summer, were golden with ripening corn
Now stand dark, and all forlorn
Hedgerows, once bedecked in green
With berries bright appear.
Swallows have flown to a warmer clime
Squirrels scamper, their winter larder to line
Chestnuts begin to fall, children with conkers play
In October, when the skies are grey,
The potato harvester, gets stuck in the mud.
While down in the lane, the brook is a flood.
As clocks go back an hour we'll gain
So I'll sit by the fire, and watch the rain.
Curl up with a book, or reminisce,
Of sun-kissed shores, with golden sands,
And cloudless, skies of blue.
When October is at hand.

Irene G Corbett

THE HUMBLE DUSTBIN

I'm just a little dustbin, standing all alone,
Nobody really likes me standing round their home.
My lid's pulled off and kicked about, of that there is no
doubt. How would you feel with your hat off, and stood up against a
water-spout?

Rubbish thrown inside and rammed home with the heel,
Gooey gunge of every kind and bits of orange peel.
The bin-man calls round once a week,
or perhaps the week after - after - after, depending how he feels.
He throws me in his dirty cart, then bangs me on the wheel,
Full of holes and dents am I, well you can imagine how I feel.

Out in the cold and dark I stand, with rubbish all around,
Then, in the dead of night, without a sound,
Ginger Tom, from next door comes crawling round,
he calls out to all his mates, 'Look here lads, see what I have found.'
He scratches at my poor old head, until he finds a juicy
meal, then, big black Bob from No 10, bites him on the heel.
He lets out such an awful squeal, then the fighting starts,
The dog joins in, *oh!* There's such an awful din,
What kind of life is this, for a poor old battered rubbish bin?
Here I lay all forlorn, the wind has spread me on the lawn,
Oh dear! Oh dear! What can I do? I know I'll end up with the flu.
All through the winter here I stand, snow and ice so close to
hand, frozen to the core am I, rubbish piled up to the sky,
And in the summer, out in the sun,
Foul smelling odour - 'cor! I don't half hum.'
Oh! I'm just a little dustbin, standing all alone,
Nobody really likes me standing round their home.

H Parker

LIFE'S AIM

How much can one be expected to give,
All the time, as long as one lives.
Nothing in return or to gain,
Is this life one lives in vain.
The mountains they get harder to climb
One is going up hill all the time.
The steeper the going, the longer the drop,
Will one fall when they reach the top,
Or will the reward be on the other side,
When one reaches their goal and peace abides.
To give and give is life's main aim,
And the rewards we receive, are not to gain.
But for happiness, to one and all,
That's life's aim, one must recall.

Ann Dimmock

NIGHT ONE

When you touched me gently with your eyes
The world outside stepped quietly away
And with melting muscles
I slipped slowly into you.

Surrounded by 'Stars'
I drift through your soft scent
Bathed in a warmth
That folds and wraps itself around me.

The smoothness of silk brushes my lips
As you breath into me,
And touching me gently with your eyes
You lead me away.

James McAuley

THE SHADOW DANCE

Within us all lies a mystery
The soul is not all that it's cracked up to be.
Equal sides are not always so
and while you're not looking the darker one grows.

Performing the dance is not shined up
and when everyone's looking the dancers are gone.
But the art of the shadow improves with need
to be one with the dark and powerful breed.

B White

UNTITLED

If you want to be a writer they say
You must write a little every day
But outside influences start creeping in
And waiting for the muse can be a pain

So often a thought just suddenly appears
And you feel you must write it down
After waiting for what seems a million years
It comes when you're shopping in town

Never mind you say as soon as we reach home
I'll put it all down on paper
But when I try to finish the poem
My thoughts just begin to taper

It's better by far
To leave it to fate
If I'm meant to be a star
All I have to do is wait.

Dorothy Miller

NAN

Do you hear us from above,
Are you sheltered
From our tears?

Life's so short,
What do you think,
When you look back,
At all those years?

Memories fading,
Like a blanket,
Left in the
Sun.

When you're born,
You're dying,
And your life has,
Just begun.

Do you see
Your daughters,
Weeping with
Your sons.

They cared for
You so much,
Their love arrived
In tons.

You left your
soul,
And slowly
Passed away.

We will love you
Forever,
And ever
And a day.

Hayley Edwards (16)

ENDING

The spiders knew it first
unmoving in their webs
the water in the well
fell and fell.
a gentle sea rolled calm
all around the earth
beneath a plumy sky
soft, so soft
the traffic of the world
slid to a trembling halt
all around the earth
the ships and trains and planes
and factory machines
slid to a grinding halt
the crowds drew close to pray
eyes bright with fears and dreams
the silken sea rolled on
so soft, so sure, so calm
beneath a plumy sky
all around the world
the spiders knew it first
they were the last to go.

Isobel Grant Stewart

RESOLUTION

Make a resolution, a ban on pollution.
Try to be thin, don't eat and you will win.
Don't be to clever, you won't live forever.
The world is a precious place.
Save it for the human race.
One day you will look down from space,
On a world gone without a trace!

A Humphrey

WHERE?

No sign of the face, or even the hand
Of God, the ultimate creator of all
And as a child in bed alone, did I call.
Till weariness whipped me into a dreamland.

Within this realm of surreal encase.
I saw physics and magic, in a dance entwine.
All that I sought, for a short while was mine.
Then lost evermore when the sun showed its face.

In my waking quest, land beneath sky.
I'd step on the dead, the failing and sick,
Searching lifelong, and preparing to die.
Begging an answer, the truth not a trick.

On my deathbed now, with breathes left afew,
I know all the answers, but leave only a clue.

At last I've shed my mortal coil,
Troubled no longer by life and its toil.
I've gained an existence
One without time.
For an unbounded awareness, death is sublime
You can have too much of a good thing, it's said,
And I look to the living,
Those returned from the dead.
Maybe I'll come back, pick up a heart,
Let a couple conceive me, in the womb a restart.
As a foetus I know, my mind will be cleared,
For to enter the living, death must be feared.

Finally I tell the truth from the lies,
The throne room of God resides in my eyes.
He's all that I see, touch, taste and hear,
What use have I then, for the feeling of fear.
This time I can love this life again found,
with God in His Heaven, and me on the ground.

Adrian Leyden

UNTITLED

You are the man I know everything about;
Someone who loves me, inside out.

I know you so well, as well as could be;
Even better in fact, than I know me.

Your beautiful face, I see each night;
Kisses me gently and whispers good night.

Your stories and excuses you don't need to sell;
For I make myself believe, every lie you tell.

I know before you, each step you will take;
Sure of the mistake you are about to make.

Your thoughts out loud, I don't need to hear;
For I can read them in your eyes, only too clear.

In you, I believe, all that I see;
I trust in our love, and all it can be.

Your name is the one I call out in fright;
As I wake up alone, in the middle of the night.

I wish I could relax, and feel content,
Oblivious and blind to the painful torment.

Ironically, the one I put above all the rest;
Was even more unfeeling, than I would ever have guessed.

The mirror reflects shattered fragments of youth;
My innocence lost, along with the truth.

The one man I know, that loves only me;
Is out again tonight, oh where can he be?

Your smile is so sweet when you turn on your charm;
Disguising any signs, that you were meaning no harm.

In your arms I always felt so safe and secure;
Having no doubts our love was for sure.

Memories we've held on to, and the love we let go;
Have made way for a new life, so, where do we go?

Thinking back on the days when our love was so strong;
Wondering what could have gone so terribly wrong.

Before we part and go our separate ways;
It's still unclear, who wins, and who pays

The one for me, he couldn't possibly be;
I didn't even know him, who was he?

You're still the one, I love now and forever,
But I'll never have you, not now and not ever!

Lisa Stanard

PRISONER

It's hot in here
All surfaces drip
With sweat and grease

I have a window
A small one
But all I get is
Blue
With the occasional white

The white offends me

My box is freedom
From the gang
From the gun
I hope it kills me

The walls reflect blackness
All blackness confined
To this box
In its place

Joseph A Sullivan

THROUGH ELEANOR'S EYES

I'm just a statue standing silent
watching life through eyes of stone,
an ever changing panorama
In this Village that's now my home.
When Edward caused my cross erected
thatched cottages clustered at my feet,
wooden carts drawn by sturdy oxen
trundled down the dusty street.
A community of working people
replaced the courts I used to grace,
my effigy, enshrined forever
in this small and pleasant place.
the seasons changed, the centuries passed,
my Village seems a timeless place,
but even in this quiet haven
progress ever kept apace.
The Bakehouse and the Blacksmith's anvil
now have gone from the Village scene,
cars and lorries bustle past me
standing on my plinth, serene.
Around my skirts the Village lingers
old stone walls of mellow hue,
the beautiful Church and bridge spanned Ise brook
ever there within my view.
What the future holds I know not,
whatever happens I'll stand on
A long dead Queen, forever remembered
in the lovely Village of Geddington.

H F Spriggs

FINEDON TOWN

Finedon Town, you know him,
She knows you, Uncle Tim,
Antique this, antique that,
One time bakery, private flat,
Old Bert shouts, 'Hello Fred,
I see your old mate is dead,'
Newer and younger it seems to me,
Indian Restaurant, well I'll be!
Once a village now a town,
that new carpark raised a frown,
In the pub's the place to be
Finedon Town, you know me!

Simon Hudson

IT'S A LOW

When you're feeling down
Wipe away that unhappy frown
And think of people worse off than you.
The abused, the frightened and the alone
The runaways unable to go home
Those with no family or relatives to care
People who are different and have to
put up with the stares.
So when you're feeling low
Think of those with nowhere to go
And remember there's no need to frown
Life is full of ups and downs.

Kelly Russell

SOMEONE WITHIN

She walked through the streets,
Stood out in the crowd
Her face made a statement
To all around.

She was different,
If only by her skin
But what's that to do
With the someone within?

But she's not just a someone,
She's one of us too
Not really any different
To me or you.

She looked at the people,
Their faces filled with hatred
She looked at the people
And waited.

For the names to begin.

Felicity M Dolby (14)

WINTER GALES

The winds that blow across the seas from Iceland
Are knocking down my fences as they blow,
And those that are still standing
Are rocking wildly, to and fro.

When the chap that says he'll come and *fix em,*
Deigns to come and *have a go*
I shall ask that *Mr Fix 'em*
To ram those fence posts
Well and truly - down below!

John G Fife

DON'T WORRY

We'll walk this path
Just the one time
So smile and laugh
And all will be fine

Sometimes that's hard
I know this is true
But your life you must guard
You only get one *you*

Bills through the letterbox
Money to be paid
You can't stop worrying
That's how you're made

The mortgage, the rent
They won't go away
Living in a tent
Would be cheaper today

Sleepless nights
Restless days
When worry bites
Life seems grey

But before you know
Your days will be done
Worries and health
Replaced sunshine and fun

Don't worry, don't panic
When those bills do arrive
Don't be sullen or manic-
At least you're alive!

Kevin Smette

THE GALLOPSMAN

Steeped in crystal-sweet morning air
that punctuates every stem,
I arm along the heath
with my imaginary friend.

I tell Him of my yearning
for that special peace,
that absolves lapsed scenes,
where had He tried to lead me,
through decades of might-have-beens.

I realise how I faulted, know why I fell,
as toe-holds became stumbles,
and footsteps I followed were cloven.
Yet when He interceded with arms outstretched
my faith and my face were hidden.

Redeemed, amended, enlightened,
I walk before you,
Divinely appointed, the Angelus sounded
I am the Gallopsman,
sent to lead with His authority,
whilst you're still inside your head.

My patriarchal role's those hollows to fill,
those mole-hills to erase,
As He charges me to make ready your track,
for that septuagenarian race.

Richard James Cornock

THROWING OUT OLD PHOTOGRAPHS

On the deep-litter principle,
eventually, something has to be done.
You cradle the Kodak pile on your lap;
the carpet will receive
the *keep* stack here; the *rejects* there.

We start with Richard's wedding
thirteen years ago.
Old friends smile out, or pose, or gesture
- glasses raised to toast bride, groom, the future.
Who, what do we throw away?

Holidays, further back in time, return.
Here we are in Cornwall,
my mother younger than I am now;
the children shivering under striped towels
No cast-offs here.

Old black and white and faded snaps
bring back the brilliant colours of past years
with 'And do you remember?' or, 'Oh look!'
How can we not treasure
deep litter?

So few rejects on the floor.
Among them picture postcards of abroad
- Bangkok pagodas; Sydney Opera House.
Easy to get rid of these.
Post them to friends.

D P C Stileman

A WISH FOR YOU

If I was granted just one wish
I would wish for a time machine,
Not to go forward in time,
For I don't wish to know what lies ahead,
But back in time.
To try and put right all the wrongs
To try and sing all the songs
That you wanted to sing.
To lift your heart
To see things as they were before
A difficult task you might say
But surely that's what wishes are for?
I still see you now
As you picked the orange blossom
From beneath the garden wall.
You turned and waved goodbye
And closed the gate.
I was left alone
To stand and watch the orange blossom petals fall.
Yes a time machine is what I wish
Not to go forward but back in time.
To try and right all our wrongs
To try and sing all those songs
That you wanted me to.
To make things as they were before.
A difficult task you might say
But surely that is what wishes are for?

Roger Stokes

ABOUT THE DROUGHT

We moan when it falls and upsets all our plans;
We groan when it doesn't and brings hose-pipe bans;
We long for a light shower of fresh cooling rain,
And dream of the day we need *macs* on again.

The river and lake beds get dried up and crack,
The Water Board chiefs face a barrage of flack;
The cornfields and woodlands are all tinder-dry,
Great caution is vital - the fire risk is high.

Drought records are broken and never before
Has there been such low rainfall - that's bad news for sure
For growers, consumers, cows, horses and sheep . . .
No rain means no growth, shortage, prices that leap!

Worse still, toxic algae forms slicks that can harm,
Despoiling our rivers and causing alarm,
Endangering animals taking a drink,
Swimmers and sailors, and oh! What a stink!

Ice-creams are on ration, life really is tough!
We don't want too much rain, but would like enough
To replenish reservoirs, so let us pray
To the One who controls all creation each day.

We may think technology answers man's need,
But can a computer give growth to a seed?
Brilliant some may be, but all power is with God
To give water from Heaven and life to the sod.

M A Sanders

THOUGHTS

As dusk begins to settle,
My thoughts stray far away,
I gaze upon an empty seat,
And bow my head and pray.
How *suddenly* and silently,
You left my side that day,
Your *last goodbye,*
A little sigh
You could not speak,
But gently weeped.
Then quietly and peacefully
In God's arms you fell asleep.
I miss you more than words can say
My love for you won't fade away.
I should not cry, but I do,
For there can never be another you.
The chain is broken, the link remains
Only God in time will repair it again.
My Token of Gratitude I will do.
May the Peace of the Lord
Be forever with you.

Selena Febeer

BRUSH STROKES

She looks her most beautiful
Having just showered,
Perched on the end of the bed,
She begins brushing her hair
With slow measured strokes,
(Forwards and backwards)
(Forwards and backwards)
I could watch her for hours.

This is true love.
Not just the chocolates and flowers,
The arguments, the tantrums,
The small talk in the small hours,
It's the little things, the simple pleasures

Someday soon I'm going to tell her,
Halt that brush in mid-stroke -
And whisper gently that I love her.

Nicholas Bain

AD VITAM AETERNUM (TO ETERNAL LIFE)

Plastic chips and plastic peas,
Makes a plastic man at ease,
He never knows, how well he fares,
Or if the real world, really cares
That he exists.

Then, as he feeds the inner man,
The transformation, once began
Goes on, and mists the vision he once saw,
Of peace and plenty ever more
For him.

Mortality his only goal,
The saving of his simple soul,
Could wait for more enticing things.
Then biting on this worldly bait,
He contemplates eternal fate
To give imagination wings
For from his pygmy past, he cries
Too late!

Pat J Farnell

JUST THE WAY YOU ARE

Some people are full of ambition
They spend their life time in constant collision, with ideas
and plans to do this and that, but after a few weeks they all fall flat.
To conquer adventures and then start anew to me it sounds just like you.

This week a golfer, then perhaps a musician,
all it would have taken is was little tuition.
Perhaps another telescope through which you can peer,
maybe some wine or even some beer.
From fancy fishes to model boats to CD ROM's and outside garden ponds.
From your DIY to your posh HI FI
It's as if you're on a quest to find something to do, something special
just for you.

Then wrapped with love in a present it came, to teach you to fly an
aeroplane.
So from engineer to pilot you became, I know it's hardly instant fame.
But you do act like a pro with all of your maps, charts and
specialised lingo.

It worried me at first when you learnt how to fly, because I though t
I would have to say
goodbye, to all the things you used to do, for they are the things I like
best about you
But you've really not changed, you're just more committed,
looking forward to going up again weather permitted.

You talk with enthusiasm to everyone you meet,
I guess it's a hobby that is kind of neat.
You scare us with plans to take us up flying,
it seems that it's not something others mind trying.
As for me, I'd rather wait, I don't want to meet with some unforeseen fate.
But I do feel proud and often say it out loud 'my dad's a pilot and he's
the best, and as for his hobbies he's more than the rest.'

One day you may even fly to another nation, but I've never been lacking in my admiration for the things you've done and will achieve, you are definitely the greatest and that I will always believe.

Sarah Walter

MOURNING MOTHER

Mourning Mother
The sun is up
Time to cry or reign again,
To wash away the pain of them

Mourning Mother
The wind is up;
It shakes against your empty cup
Do I fill it or do I not?

Mourning Mother
It's a lovely day
The birds are singing
And children play
But the tunes of few
Are carried away
By the ear you quietly keep for they

Mourning Mother
You're tired once more
I shall pray for your healing
While I kneel in awe
At the beauty you exude
On the way to the gate
And I fear for all
Who maybe too late.

Dominic Brumwell

THE COW

I went on down to the shops one day.
I just popped out for a bite . . .
. . . and then when I arrived back home
I got a terrible fright.

The dog had eaten all the cat food
and the cat was saying 'bow-wow'!
I didn't know it then you see,
but I was followed home by a cow.

The cow did a tap dance
right next to the bin
Then she looked at me and said
'You're looking terribly thin.'

She cooked me up an omelette
and a lovely apple pie.
I asked her was she staying long
and she cheerily winked her eye.

Cow and I became best friends
and I didn't want her to go
Then one morning when I was fast asleep
I heard a noise in the street below.

What a surprise when I opened my eyes
and saw cow with her own café.
I leaped up and down
            and jumped for joy
'Hooray, cow's here to stay.'

Helen Eldridge

NOT JUST A FRIEND

Please let me tell you all about my very special friend -
She is a lady, oh so grand, who I'll love to the end!
I remember as a small girl she would sit me on her knee -
and wipe away my tears so no-one else would see.

She'd comfort me when I was ill and nurse me back to health
and her heart of gold is worth more than riches and wealth.
Like a shining light she guided me through my teenage years
with all the problems they bring she always eased my fears.

As I grew into a woman, there she was right by my side -
my admiration and respect for her I really just cannot hide.
She has stood by me religiously when times were really bad
and a more moving, caring friend no-one has ever had!

She is a lady full of grace even though she's sixty nine,
the older she gets, the better, just like a bottle of wine!
She'll stand no nonsense and one respects her standards and rules
A bit on the stubborn side she can be and gladly suffers no fools!

I don't know how, I don't know when but I hope there'll be a day
when all the love she has shown to me I can start to repay.
It will take me all of my lifetime and many more years as well
to thank her for her *deeds of kindness* that are too numerous to tell!

Folk around say we're alike and with this I must agree -
for the resemblances we have to each other is very plain to see!
Now I'll let you into my secret - I think the time has come
to tell you that my special friend is really *my dear mum!*

Lesley White

THE GREYHOUND AND TORTOISE

You have probably heard of the hare and tortoise race
If you haven't, well, this is similar in any case
This time, the tortoise is matched alongside a greyhound
A fast, formidable creature I'll be bound
At the start, the greyhound is eager, pawing at the door of his trap
While the tortoise is real laid back, chewing at a lettuce leaf scrap
The race begins and the greyhound *disappears* leaving behind him
a cloud of dust
In which the poor tortoise coughs and splutters much to his disgust
The greyhound races into a sports stadium and sprinters he overtakes
And to show off, five laps of the track in total, he makes
He delights in being able to run fast
And to kick back dust at those he runs past
Leaving the arena, he runs ahead far
Then for a short rest, calls in at a Karaoke bar
Barking and howling to *You ain't nothing but a hound dog* and others
besides
He finishes his slush puppy drink and runs back outside
Thinking the tortoise must be getting quite near
He runs back to the course where the spectators cheer
However, as a source of gambling, he wonder what he's bet
As into a betting shop he goes where all the punters sweat
Some of them try to catch him but he gives them the slip
Yet he collides with a table leg, causing him to trip
Back on the course again, he sees with alarm, down the street
That the tortoise is about to break the finishing tape, which would mean
his defeat
In response, he sort of half runs, half trots, willy nilly
Because the collision with the table leg sort of knocked him silly
Too late, the tortoise claims victory, as the tape he breaks through
And he wins his prize of the day, Hackney Greyhound Racing,
tickets for two.

D J Furnell

BILLY SWAILES

When I was a lad and lived with me' Dad
We sat by the fire telling tales,
And my favourite of all the ones I recall,
Was the story of young Billy Swailes.

With Dad on his stool, and me at his knee
I'd look up at him and he'd look down on me
Then he'd say, now this story (and his eyes would go sad)
Is about the best friend that a boy ever had.

See when I was a boy in the village of Skalls
Me and young Billy Swailes were the greatest of pals.
All thru' the long summers of boy browning sun,
Together we'd laugh - together we'd run,
And catch the wild butterfly or furious bee
Together forever Billy and me.

We had castles of haystacks - mountains of bricks
Bracken built caves and weapons of sticks.
And hours spent just swinging from the bough of some tree
'Cos life was for living for Billy and me.

But one day when playing he said to me, Tom,
What will you do when they tell you I've gone.
And I didn't understand what he was trying to say.
But I never saw Billy again from that day
'Cos his mother came round and weeping she said
That poor Billy Swailes at eleven was dead.
And his last words still haunt me these distant years on,
What will you do, when they tell you I've gone.

Kevin Eustace

A CHILD'S PERSPECTIVE

Red wellies and ruddy cheeks
moist with rain and exertion,
wear a smile at the door.
Dimpled fingers clasp rhubarb trees
canopied beneath the leaves.

'What have you got Joseph? I ask.
shoulders shrug a gleeful smile
matching mine -
a pair of twinkling eyes.
'I've got rhubarbs!' His reply.

'What can you do with it?' I enquire.
'I can do that!' says Joe
holding two sticks in various poses
of semaphore.
My eyes turn green at his rose-coloured
glasses.

Lined up side by side
red-coated soldiers stand and hide
beneath the canopy of green
through a child's perspective seen
He would never guess that I
would want to cook them in a pie

Lord, in my vision make me humble
not all I see is rhubarb crumble!

Chrissy Smith

TOMORROW IS SO FAR AWAY

I've loved you in vain for a long time,
I know that's the price I must pay,
You say you will love me tomorrow,
But tomorrow is so far away.

Your eyes show the fear of a stranger,
of someone who you never knew,
You say you were hurt in your springtime,
A heart-ache that I've been through too.

I've loved you in vain for a long time,
I know that's the price I must pay,
You say you will love me tomorrow,
But tomorrow is so far away.

You needed the love of a lifetime,
And no other lover would do,
But memories fade in the sunshine
And we'll start our summer anew.

I've loved you in vain for a long time,
I know that's the price I must pay,
You say you will love me tomorrow,
But tomorrow is so far away.

Your longing for loving is over,
You know what you have to do,
Just forget the pain of your springtime,
I'll spend autumn and winter with you.

I've loved you in vain for a long time,
I know that's the price I must pay,
You say you will love me tomorrow,
But tomorrow is so far away.

James Whitehead

THROUGH A CHILD'S EYES

Oh to see life again through a child's eyes.
I once saw the world so clearly.
Each hour was welcomed as another play
on a stage I loved so dearly.
Rainbow-coloured days of chocolate and
lemonade; rolling hoop; skipping-rope and
kite.
Rummaging in Granny's bag on her weekly visit, an
Aladdin's cave of delight.
Blowing out candles on birthday cakes.
Bright balloons, laughter warm and merry.
Hanging up stockings for Santa Claus to fill . . . remembering of
course his glass of sherry.
Milk teeth hidden under pillow for the
fairies to build ivory homes; they always left a new shiny
threepence, and sometimes a sweet from the gnomes.

Age should bring wisdom and maturity they say.
But I can't say I feel very wise.
The passing years stole my treasures away.
My world I no longer recognise.
The grass doesn't grow as green in the glade.
Stars have lost that certain twinkle in the skies.
And given the chance my all would I trade to see
life, once again, through a child's eyes.

Ira Saunders

ABSENCE

I love this room with its peace
And its isolation.
Even its very pink-ness
Fails to annoy.
It is here, where I close my eyes
And see your face beside me.
Here, wrapped in silence,
Where I remember your words,
And the touch of your hands
On my skin.
On the crumpled sheets beneath me
Your scent still lingers.
And wrapped in your presence,
I sleep.

Zoë Sutton

SONNET

In the life that we live, dying is not
the final curtain; there is but more there,
just the other side of death; that is where
the soul is truly alive. Wanting not
for material wealth but gaining love.
Death cannot be the end of existence;
it is the beginning of innocence.
Meeting with those we've lost, already above.
The way forwards through the dark becomes clear
as we drift into a new realm of calm.
No time for fond farewells and futile tears;
the journey's end will not be cold but warm
and safe, surrounded by love, free from fear.
Don't be afraid. To die is to be reborn.

Emma Montgomery

LITTLE BIG BOY

To-day it is a battlefield,
tomorrow it's a farm,
One day it's a raging sea, in seconds it is calm.
It could be my favourite car, going very fast,
or maybe it's a pirate ship, I'm look-out up the mast!
It becomes a castle, with soldiers of all sorts,
or I could be a big rich King, and this one of my forts.
Grown-ups who come walking by don't seem to understand,
They just seem to smile and see,
A simple box of sand.
'Please Mum'
Please don't put the light out mum, I know that you are there,
but when it goes all quiet and dark, all things start to scare,
There's monsters, snakes and spiders too and if I start calling you,
you will say Oh! Go to sleep, everything's alright.'
But I cannot go to sleep, especially at night.
There's lots of things which I don't like, to bring me tears or sorrow,
Please leave the light on, just tonight,
and I'll grow up tomorrow!

Jim Keen

DAUGHTER OF MINE

Not like me
inner voice sighs.
Hard being me
insecure upon lies.

She is not me
Strong identity -
Knows her mind
owns a soul
safe and sure
heads for goal.

Has not my fears, Thank God.
Had not to tread
where I had trod.

Another Saturday's child
working hard for a living.
Like me, but then
she's got more giving.
She is not me, it is true.
Alike, yes sure, but better too.

Lynn Linsell

TALL GRASSES

Cocksfoot, fescue, timothy and rye
Stand at the gravestones shoulder high,
Shrouding, this shimmering, clover-sweet June,
Each simple legend and village rune.

Then, as June ends and ripeness follows,
And the air is filled with new-winged swallows,
And the grass is mown for hay-time yield,
The lichened memories are revealed.

When sailor William sat on the throne,
Died plain John Smith, his life's course run:
Also, 'Dearly Beloved, his Relict, Joan
Called home together; Thy will be done.'

So others down the corridor of years,
Humbly recall their brevity of tears;
While for passing shades the grass grows high,
Fescue, timothy, cocksfoot and rye.

Alan Poole

ALL CONSUMING LOVE

I stand in the park surrounded by trees,
some thick and sturdy, some thin in stature.
The leaves are oceans of rich greens and deep burnt browns, they sway
and dance as the wind sends a gentle breeze through them.

I stand in the park.
I feel the gentle breeze sweep softly through my hair
and smile as it cools my heated brow.

I stand in the park.
My heart is singing a silent song along with the nightingales that nest
high up in the trees.
My whole body is filled with electrifying sensations, I remember this
morning you told me you loved me.

I stand in the park.
I listen to the wind as it rustles through the trees.
My thoughts are consumed by the miracle of your love for me.
Never again will I feel such deep loneliness and desolation.
I am no longer an empty vessel, your love has made me whole.
No river, no distance,
no other person will ever be able to destroy the love of two souls that
have joined together to become one person.

I stand under a big oak tree.
Out of the corner of my eye I see a darting rabbit.
A lone pigeon sits pecking at the grass.
I close my eyes your face appears before me.
Your deep penetrating eyes,
your handsome chiselled features
and pitch black hair makes my heart flutter.
I take a deep sighing breath.
Oh to be loved and feel such love is wonderful.

Pearl Robinson

CHILDHOOD MEMORIES

When the water in the jug and bowl
Froze on the marble top
And part of every bedroom scene
Was a matching china pot.

The only central heating then
Was a round hot-water bot
Of shiny aluminium
When into bed one got

And if you were - well - *well-off*
You had the *electric* on
Then you fumbled in the darkness
'Cos the shilling's worth had gone

For the most of us it was gaslight
On a bracket on the wall
Which sent the shadows dancing
As the pressure did rise and fall.

When you scrubbed every morning washday
In a galvanised washing bath
With a scrubbing board and a laundry brush
And you swept off the front step and path

Then you black-leaded grates and beat carpets
And you chopped sticks the fire for to lay
And your stockinged feet slid on the lino
Which you swept, mopped and polished each day

Some will say the old days are the good ones
But I'd rather my car and my freezer
Hot water and dishwasher, tele and shower,
Than a tin bath, cold water, and geyser!

Elsie Hill

JOE

Poor old Joe,
Alone all day long he sits in his chair,
No-one he knows has time to spare.
His life is passing, the years have flown,
Now he spends so much time on his own.
Books surround him, his only escape,
Covered with dust, like the coals in the grate.
The door bell rings, he rises to see,
Who he wonders has come to see me.
Slowly he finally reaches the door,
Whoever it was had gone long before.
He stands there gazing into space,
Fatigue and despair showing on his face.
Slowly he returns to his fireside chair,
No-one he knows has time to spare.
He stares at the furniture and carpets all worn,
His home, like him, is neglected and forlorn.
His life is so empty and soon he'll be gone.
Then there'll be nothing where he belonged.
All things must turn to dust and decay,
By the natural course they will all blow away.
Nature then shakes the dust from her feet,
Evolving onward, her task complete.
The breathing life force continues to evolve
As ever this planet on its axis revolves.
Poor Old Joe.
All day long he sits in his chair,
No-one he knows has time to spare.

Carole Wood

THE SINGLES CLUB

The untogether all together
In a relationship, doing what they will
When they can (given the chance of course)
With no rebounds of love
Except for the few.
Their bewildered thoughts
And actions of the lonely.
Which, although is hiding,
Can be seen through a two way mirror
Which has cracked a long time ago
But still gets a weekly polish
To confirm it still has a use
Though the crack really
Is just another broken heart.

Nick Jones

UNTITLED

The soft, windswept days of yesteryear,
How I wish they could greet me here
Every moment frozen, in my fragile, egg shell mind
Days of limitless glee, sunshine thoughts so kind
I remember the day the light faded and my smile finally cracked
Lost, youth-filled life the world became heart attack black
The time of loss turned into a fruitless search for answers
Life was replaced with tragic tales and lonely, helpless dancers
Years have passed on too and memories painfully fade
I look around me and you and the love kept in the shade
I have woken still sleepy from the woeful, wasted haze
Is this the sun that I see, will it brighten up these days?
The smile from this *son* is brighter than a million stars
Joy I once denied has opened up my scarred dormant heart.

Thank you, I owe my life to you!

Mark Mason

UNTITLED

Why do I cry when I hear children's voices
Calling out in the still of a crisp winter morning?
I remember the days, far away in time and place;
The days when I felt my whole life was dawning.

The voices sing out, I hear laughter and innocence,
The house is their country, the garden their universe,
Troubles are transient, forgiveness near instant,
No knowledge have they that their lives will be worse.

To me there was always sun, or better still, snow,
The rain, a diversion, in which to float boats
Or splash wellies; never the grey veil
Which makes me now shudder and turn up the collar of my coat.

Now as I sit here torn apart from my home
The memories of sunshine drift back through the years.
I may scorn at the happiness, the ignorance, the child,
But it's hard for my heart not to ache with my tears.

S Prest

LEARNING

Life is as precious as the time you are here,
Meaning use to your fullest advantages,
Thinking always positive . . . never negative,
Experience subjects throughout your finest ages.

Crossing paths of ancestral mystery,
Learning methods of peoples of the past,
Gaining knowledge by the opening of secrets,
Forever studying to be sure we are not the last.

Stephen Grant Lamonby

CHILDHOOD DAYS

What can you remember about your childhood days?
For one thing it was always hot it hardly ever rained.
And if it did we kids were told to 'put your wellies on'
Up and down the street we'd go dragging one foot in the gutter,
sloshing all the rain in puddles, that made mother mutter.

Skipping ropes stretched in the road the old rhymes come to
mind, spinning tops sent whirling thrashed with the leather
whip straight into the marble game, then we'd get some stick.

The three-wheeled bike was the best of all, pedalling like
fury to get up a speed with your best friend perched on
the back, scooters didn't compare they just couldn't
compete as we skidded and screeched our way down the street.

Ah yes those were the days, Sunday school, youth clubs, the
like; what have we now *video games* I'd swap for my old
three-wheeled bike.

W Welch

TEACHER TROUBLE

The trouble with teachers
Is they think they're so smart
Telling us what to do in Maths and Art

The lessons are boring
Especially Geography
But every lesson really
Is like a bedtime story

But I reckon they try
To make it good
But they don't try to make it
As good as they could.

Alan Winn (9)

SHOEING THE GOOSE

I'm carrying coals where they don't need to go,
Rolling water in barrels along with the flow,
What the deuce -
I'm shoeing the goose.

Piling papers on desks where they'll topple and fall,
Sending messages where they'll do no good at all,
Staying loose -
Only shoeing a goose.

When rallying, tallying, setting forth sallying,
I pause in the doorway and start dilly-dallying,
By Zeus!
Must be shoeing the goose.

Those who sweat, strain and labour
Do never Life savour,
They would think it *odd*
Were a goose ever shod.

I'm quite content really to muddle on through.
There's always a limit to what you can do.
What's your excuse?
Shoeing the goose?

Penelope Alexander

UNTITLED

You are my strength when I am weak
You are my thoughts when I can not speak
You make me smile when I am down
You make me realise I am not alone

You make me laugh when I want to cry
You are gentle and strong at the same time
You protect me from harm and keep me safe
You make my life fun to live

You have made me see
You have made me feel
You have reached inside and freed my soul
You have taken my pain away

No-one has done any of this before
No-one gives a second look
No-one realises I am blind.

L Wyles

EARTHED

Every year
the woman waited for her
ancient apple tree to bloom.
The moment the first pink and white
blossoms appeared she sighed with
relief, now everything would
be all right. Then, last
Spring, a terrible gale
uprooted the apple
tree and the young
flowers withered.
That
night
she
died
in
her
sleep

Geraldine Newbrook

REFUGEES

Dragging feet, shuffling along an unknown road,
Dull eyes deadened by life-long fear,
Blank faces, suspiciously regarding authority,
For authority killed their loved ones;
Drove them from their homes to wander in a foreign land,
To shelter in cardboard shacks provided by some friendly organisation,
Trudging desolately away, leaving all they know,
Clutching their few possessions pathetically bundled together.
Children squalling, frightened, families fleeing
With their lives held in the hand of warriors.
Here are the sufferers from the senseless wars,
The remainders of war's destruction,
The ones who are perpetual reminders
Of all that man creates in order to destroy . . .
The hopeless ones . . . the refugees.

D M Kemp

ESSENCE

A child talking to her dead mother.
The soft whisper of the departed lover.
Spirits that hover, encircling our very being,
All around us listening, feeling and seeing.

Our world is amongst the visionary realm.
We are actors on a mortal's film,
each body playing out its crucial part,
the flickering of essence in the heart.

The small spark glimmering while await,
for only the good knows the fate.
The spark will journey to the fire.
To an eternity that will never tire.

Sherree Dudley

PENNY

Out of the mint I came shining and new
And placed in a bank along with a few
I was put in a pocket of a man unknown
Then in a shop till I was thrown
A small boy put me in a box
And for a while I was forgot
A few more pennies joined me there
Then to a shop we went together
After that I was dropped in a drain
And washed along by the rain
On a pavement I came out
And picked up by a boy scout
Over time the places have varied
In and out where I have been carried
Quite dirty and soiled I now lay
In a garden deep in clay.

Gilian Bichard

MY MUM

My Mum with her bright freckly skin,
Has sparkling green eyes and is rather thin.
When my Mum is happy she smiles down at me,
When she is sad she loses her key.
My Mum is kind, gentle and fun,
Her favourite thing is to be in the sun.
My Mum works across the grey, dirty street,
You can hardly call that tiring for her feet.
She cooks all our wonderful meals.
Her favourite animals are the grey friendly seals.
Unfortunately she's allergic to anything with fur,
But from now on I'm going to try to be as nice as her.

Juliet Gillett (13)

TO CARLY . . . THE LITTLE GIRL IN THE PORTRAIT

She looks the picture of innocence
Sparkling eyes and winsome smile,
A barefoot girl in Victorian dress
Captured for a while
In a time, one hundred years ago
When life was not so fast,
When there was time to stand and watch
As life went slowly past.

As she gazes through dreaming eyes
Does she wonder what it was like
To be a little Victorian girl
And live in that far off time,
To always be hampered by long frilly skirts
A beribboned hat on her hair
In place of the jeans and trainers
Today's children normally wear.

Will she look back as the years go by
And remember the little girl
Who stepped right back for a moment in time
To her great - great - grandmother's world?

Edna Cosby

TABBY

Tail-tipped tiger,
Sleek and sinuous
You sat
          Amid the tulips.

You, tabby with talons,
Called truce on
Enticing movements
And sat
          Statuesque:

Drinking life's sunshine -
Its warmth and serenity.

I sank into obvious relaxation
But you? - no -

The dark slits in pale green
Kept watch -
over your domain.

Linda M Norris

WISHES

My hour will come, I believe
Although I find it hard to
I somehow see a gold glimmer
But it may just disappear
I will see it one day and then
I will be in total happiness
He touches me and loves me
My heart sings with utter bliss
he is my dream, I am his
This is all I really live for
Or else my life would be
Misery like it used to be
My existence is like gold
And he says he loves me to death
I used to be sad and lost
How you have fulfilled me
he says the same but it is
Just there, no little questions
We wished it would, it has
To be born for and to die for.

Sara Richardson

UNTITLED

Put me in a binbag
When I pass away
I really don't mind at all
'Cos where I'm put I'll stay.

They come on Thursday morning you know
In their Phoenix truck
So throw me up in the back
I'll be undiscovered, with a bit of luck.

It's reassuring to know you see
That body cares at all!
In this time of monitory cuts
To economise with the funeral

If the council should complain
Saying 'It's not our job mate
To cart away late personages
'Tis a job we really hate.'

The journey out wasn't too bad
The truck was really rather cosy
The in-flight meal was garbage though
And pedestrians are rather nosey

And now the moon is going down
Over that council tip
It really is quite nasty here
I don't think it was worth the trip!

Steve Eaton

PATHWAY IN THE PARK

The sun is shining on this nice warm spring day
My dog at my side as we walk through the park-way
New grass growing beneath my feet,
Flowers coming to see above.

As we walk along the pathway smelling different
fragrances of plants and earth
One imagines the flowers blooming
and racing to get through first.

The tall trees which have weathered the rain and storms
To stretch out their branches
Reaching up as if been re-born.
From daffodils roses daisies and more blooms to come.

Just like people when their patch is disturbed
they close their leaves in alarm
It doesn't take much to feel alive walking
through a park underneath a clear blue sky.

The nice cool breeze on your face
listening to the tall trees swaying,
Knowing it's nature you respect as all year round
You have something different to see, as parks are never failing.

Leigh

THE BATTLE OF NASEBY

In sixteen hundred and forty five, in Naseby's neighbourhood,
Englishmen faced Englishmen, as enemies they stood
In a savage civil war which they felt they had to fight
To preserve the precious tenets they all believed were right.

Gay Cavaliers were for King Charles - their blood was tinged with blue,
While Roundheads of much humbler stock to Cromwell's cause were true.
On confrontation that June morning, before fighting for their lives,
They thought of tousled children, their families and wives.

A whispered prayer and a flickering fear fluttered along the ranks
Of Royalists and Commoners, who promised God their thanks
If they survived the carnage that for them on this day loomed,
But many soldiers shed a secret tear knowing that they were doomed.

The generals of both armies sought ground both dry and high
And deployed their men on ridges, resolved to do or die.
Valiant Skippon manned the centre with Cromwell on his right,
On the left bold Henry Ireton - Fairfax was ready for the fight.

Charles led his men in person, with breastplates shining bright,
Langdale's horsemen on his left, brave Prince Rupert at his right.
Towards eleven in the morning, they advanced with purpose grim
And Cromwell called upon the Lord to guide and succour him.

At first Rupert's charging troopers made the Ironsides give ground,
But Cromwell's waves of cavalry turned the battle round
To break the lines of Cavaliers and force them to retreat,
By one o'clock they fled the field, ragged in defeat.

There were five thousand prisoners and seventeen hundred slain,
The King lost all his infantry, his guns and baggage train.
When the conflict ended, to Roundheads' eternal shame,
They massacred camp followers and tarnished their good name.

And women wept as their loved ones slept the peaceful sleep of the dead
But at least the spirits of those in cold repose had no more battles to dread.
Historians say, that on that day, the Divine Right of Kings was overthrown
And in the blood-soaked soil of Naseby, the seeds of our Parliament
were sown.

John Martin

WHITHER MANKIND?

Are there, within mankind, inherent aspirations
Which makes him ever doubt the gift of life?
Can he stand, full square, to fulfil his obligations,
Exposed to troubles, also facing strife?

People look for captains, thus adopt them for their need
They trust in each to lead them all the way,
But human strengths can crumble, or may be obsessed by greed,
Thus regulations seldom hold their sway.

Every race will find that imperfections block the road
Thus search for peerless aid to make life flow;
Some seek idols, thunder, stars or sun to ease their load,
Or mystic acts to make their life-blood glow.

Letting money be a god may lead to selfish lust,
And churlish deeds inhibit tender love.
In what power, then, may earthlings in their hearts bestow their trust,
Reject such thoughts? - Or look for help above?

Strangely, whilst denying power, subconscious voices plead
'God Bless,' 'Thank God,' 'God help me in my plight,'
And at life's end serenity can soothe a soul in need,
With trust that darkness can be turned to light.

Ted Grove

THE ARTHRITIC

She sits in her chair as still as a mouse
No more her footsteps can be heard in the house
Nature has claimed her as one of his victims
After years of activity now lots of restrictions

She has to sit still dreaming of days past
But thanks God she has memories to last
The many years she may have to sit there
By the big window in her special chair.

She could see all the flowers the birds in the trees
Where once she walked happily in the breeze
Doing her jobs around the place
Now inactivity she has to face.

She thought of years gone so much going on
Children born children crying children singing and sometimes dying

Where had they gone those years so sweet
Oh for the sound of footsteps in the street
To let her know she hadn't been forgotten
For no more could she go to see her dear ones
She had to sit and wait and hope on.

We are born to many joys and sorrows
But it's hard to have to live with your tomorrows
When nature frail as it sometimes is
Takes away our blessings and has nothing more to give
Than sickness pain and inert limbs
So on they sit and to their memories cling.

L Bird

I NEED TO BE ALONE

I need to be alone today. A few hours would do.
There is a place I remember, not far from Cublington,
Near where I bought some trees some time ago.
There is so much to do at home.
I've been hanging patterned paper till my arms and mind
Are weary. Paint sticks in my nose and clogs my finger nails.
I'm bored with plumblines, nails and screws.
My neck is cricked with painting ceilings
And my hair is hard with plaster's dust.
Today I will leave it all.
I shall go to Cublington and find that place,
Take a paper, a drink, my old folding chair.
There I shall sit and read the Telegraph,
While all around the wind hushes through the trees.
Maples, birch, oak and ash which grateful locals placed
In thanks, that airport schemes of yesteryear were trashed.
Such peace, save the odd passing car.
The warming sun creates dappled shadows in the long grass.
Silver fairies float and flirt, birds chirp unseen.
It must be good to be a bird. No burdens, no concerns.
I love it, but I cannot stay too long.
I have responsibilities. I still have jobs to finish,
New ones to start. Shelves to fix, floors to lay,
Lights to change, bills to pay.
The birds I shall leave to their place.
I shall come again another day,
I found peace if only for a few hours.

Jim Hetterley

THE HOLE

So there was this hole - empty!
A big, round, empty hole, dead centre of the lawn.
Been there ever since we moved in.
I'd wanted a fancy wishing well -
Charlie had wanted a tree.
Never could agree about nothing.
Spent the last twenty years arguing we had.
Argue, argue, argue, for twenty years.
Talk of the village we were.
Then last week Charlie said he'd had enough.
'I'm off!' he said.
He told all the village he was going
So they weren't surprised on Friday
When I said he'd gone.
'Off to his sister up north,' I told them.

On Saturday Mr Perkins came to build the well.
Nice man Mr Perkins, a widower, very obliging.
I always did like him.
He's made a nice job of it, looks very attractive
From the kitchen window, quite a striking feature.

It's got an echo too.
Me and Mr Perkins tried it out this morning,
Leant over the side and yelled,
'Hope you like the well, Charlie!'
Echo came back a bit indistinct, but there,
We never did agree about nothing.

J Williams

TIME TICKS BY

Have you ever sat and watched time tick by?
The seconds beat rhythmically in your head
The seconds turn to minutes, hours
What are you thinking?

Is someone dying?
Is someone crying?
Is a new life beginning?
Is there joy in the world?

Silence surrounds you
Just the beat of time to be heard
Like a heartbeat, it strums on

How long have you been sitting here now?
Has someone fallen in love?
Has someone lost their love?
Is someone hoping, praying?

How much time has gone by?
How much time has been wasted?
Wasted by us!
Enough time to help others!
Support others!
Pray for others!
Listen to others!
Enough time to help the world and each other

Samantha Hulston

MEMORIES OF LUTON

I ride the grey suburban streets with houses built like boxes,
That once were fields and countryside that were havens for the foxes
And other wildlife swept away, now that the hedgerows are no more
No fields of corn in the breezes sway, for the streets of town reach to their door.
Gone is the chalk blue butterfly that danced on Dallow Down
And all the other chalky hills that surround Luton Town,
For now those hills are buried deep 'neath countless bricks and mortar
That went to build the houses for John Doe, his wife and daughter.
The hamlets and villages that once existed separately,
Now merge into that sprawling place as if they never used to be
Once linked by country lanes to town they blend in road by road,
And all that makes them different is the district postal code.
At night from the top of Longcroft Hill, as far as the eye can see,
Stretch necklaces of golden lights where farmyards used to be
Like sparkling webs of shining lace
They stretch for miles, from place to place,
No glow-worms these, they light the way
To show the size of the town today.
Shrill whining from the airport and the buzz of motorway,
Replace the songs of skylarks each hour of the day
Yet though we long nostalgically
For the times and places that used to be
There's no going back - we must go on.
For the sake of others that follow on
We have to build and plan so the town
Continues to grow, and doesn't go down
To become an empty soulless place
Where no-one knows their neighbour's face
And as long as all our memories last
We can look to the future whilst honouring the past.

Joyce Nunn

LAMENT OF DECEMBER INSPECTOR OF TAXES

On frost-shaved fields
Listless sun cuts out
Cardboard sheep and cattle,
Stocked in their shadows -

In my room are stacked cabinets
Of districts, sliced sheaves of paper,
Each head and tree noted,
Mine for milking for you -

But the scallywag rooks and crows
Fly jeering at my eyes, so I blink
And lose the picture -

The damn birds pay no taxes!

Ali Cohen

MIDNIGHT SUN

When the midnight sun comes out to play
She puts you and I asleep for a day.
The sky dresses up in a formal black,
And she wears stars of night upon her back.
Honoured guests are but few,
the owl, the cat, the kiwi,
But not you.
They dance to the music of the howling wind
And listen to the songs of the rustling trees
They drink from pools of midnight rain,
And eat their fill from bowls of grain
And when the sun no longer plays
They thank you not for the light of day.

E M Cawte

POWER IN THE HEAVENS

Far mightier than a shining sword
Far brighter than a flash
of a camera, with such magnitude,
that precedes the mighty crash.

The lightning strikes, the thunder roars,
This! No-one can control,
No orders can be issued,
No government has this role.

With the wonder of the heavens
under which we often cower,
Against the fiercest storms that rage,
Mere humans have no power.

If life on earth were threatened
from an unknown source above,
Only then would nations stand together,
United in peace and love.

Betty Warner

THE MAGPIE

Alone you doom me, or so they all say,
In pair you promise a fruitful new day,
Your flash of white feathers borne within black,
As upon the wing you alter your track,
I have long wondered, it makes me think,
Between you and fortune, is there a link?
Your famed evil as you swoop from the sky,
Can this all be true? My friend, the magpie.

Tony Reason

REMEMBER ME,
ETERNALLY YOURS

W hy does it always seem to be,
A nother one passing straight by me.
Y ou know the chance I stood with you,
N ever existed what could I do.
E ternally yours.

F orever close this experience of jail, for
O ver in my mind it will turn,
S weet thoughts of you will fill my head,
T ouching me, with loving concern.
E ternally yours,
R emember me?

D Williams

JOURNEY INTO THE SOUL

Me, a person I'm trying to get to know,
I have stumbled onto the path,
Uncertain of how far I must go,
To find the glow that lies deep within -
To discover the natural me,
To discard the conditioned ideas and feelings
which are not my own,
To rip away the flesh and bone,
To find my core, tear it free
And learn what makes me think and feel.
This journey I must ride alone,
with only my soul on board,
Confusion may run me off the road,
But my thirst will drive me on,
Until I reach and touch my goal,
A union of flesh and soul.

L J Hobbs

INTO MY WORLD

Into my world,
into my easy world
something desperate comes.
Not dressed in comfortable clothes,
but ancient cast-offs, visibly soiled,
shuffling down-at-heel across the floor,
he enters uninvited
as welcome as a leper at the wedding feast.
And from the voluminous folds
of his teeming coat
a million images slide out,
of starving children, thin flesh,
staring eyes, wasted bone,
skin and death.
An embarrassment that will not let us eat
our meal in peace,
a mangy dog that keeps on straying back,
he will not leave.

He will not leave.

David Read

DARKNESS

Darkness surrounds me
I know not why.
But I shall not sit and cry
I'll walk along this tunnel today
for tomorrow I will see the light of day.
And when that light
comes shining through,
I'll know I have pulled myself through.

Dianne Johnson

THE DAYS OF OUR LIVES
LIVE TO DIE

There'll be days in the sun full of pleasure and fun
When your engine's well serviced and oiled
There'll be days dull and cold you'll feel haggard and old
When the spring in your step has recoiled
There'll be days of your youth you're convinced of a truth
Before wisdom is yours as of yet
There'll be days you won't want to remember
Full of memories you'd rather forget
There'll be days when you don't heed the warnings
Then live to regret what you've said
There'll be days you get up in the mornings
When you'll wish you had stayed in your bed
There'll be days when you feel rather pleased with yourself
When your talent emerges and shines
There'll be days when you'd rather be anywhere else
Than the place where you're at at the time
There'll be days when you don't feel on top of your form
And all you can hope for is rest
There'll be days when you can't do what has to be done
Just as long as you have done your best
There'll be days when the hours just aren't long enough
They get shorter as years roll on by
There'll be days when you'll wonder why life is so tough
When you get there just get up and fly
Through the days you determine enough is enough
Of complaining and questioning why
Every day is a gift we should treasure as if
It's the first or our last - live to die.

Anne Dunn

THE OLD TOWN HALL

I think about our lovely town,
When I was very small.
Where, in the high street, proud as punch,
There stood the old town hall.

The steps were wide, to get inside
Onto its polished floor,
With meetings, dances, concerts held
Behind its solid door.

It towered o'er the market,
Which then, came twice a week,
And watched the shoppers who had come,
Some bargains for to seek.

Upon its splendid balcony,
When voting day was here,
The victor stood acknowledging
The crowd's triumphant cheer.

Then progress said - the town must change,
We had no chance at all,
And I recall the fateful time
We lost our *old town hall.*

I E Crumley

THE CHILDREN

Children are noisy when they are at play
Shouting and laughing, as they join the fray
Swinging and sliding, jumping to and fro
Joining in everything, till it's time to go.

Holding hands with father, what a day they've had
They shout, 'You'll bring us here tomorrow, won't you Dad?'
He smiles, a little wearily, and nods, I'll come
And soon the happy little band are safely home.

The talk in bed dies down, Dad takes a peep
Their mother tiptoes out, 'Hush, they're fast asleep'
It's not easy, caring for children all the time
It's good to see them growing up, and in their prime.

The girls grow up so quickly, the boys just take time slow
Until they venture into sport, then it's all up and go
Football, cricket and rugby, good sports, that's the truth.
All these things our children need, to enjoy their youth.

M Turner

SUMMER

After spring had awoken us,
Summer sauntered in slowly.
Up where the gulls and swallows flew,
The sun became serious and aeroplanes left white messages of hope.
The bees busied themselves with the flowers;
Bloom after bloom of Van Gogh colours.
Butterflies balanced on buddleia.
Bindweed became rampant with its purple and white flowers
Winking at us; goading us for our lack of weeding.
Summer exuded sexuality with bare bronzed limbs
And flowers in our hair.
Back doors left open, windows ajar;
No boundaries now between outside and inside.
Cats sprawled even sleepier and dogs despaired.

Time passed;

We yawned;

Time passed.

William Robert Greig

THE FRIGHTENED BOY

While the skipping ropes turned, as the children played,
While the excited cries rang out, when the children charged around,
And the teachers chattered and drank cups of tea,
The frightened boy cowered in the corner.

And the bully approached, and the child shrank smaller,
And raised his hands to his face, and his heart pounded faster,
And he screamed for help, but was all alone,
The bully got closer.

And the bully arrived, and the teachers turned away,
And the boy screamed for attention, and cried in fear,
And he heard the bell ring and the people left, but the bully stayed,
And as he fought for his life, and shouted more,
No-one came.

Catherine-Dawn Brudenell

MY LOVE FOR HIM

My heart is aching with pain,
My love has gone,
You've journeyed to another woman,
As I have not given you pleasure,
Only by listening I understand you,
But your desires I cannot reach,
I love you, want to cherish you,
Hold you, touch you,
Give you fantasies to desire,
Let you love me, kiss me,
And do everything with me,
I seem to love you in mind,
But fear your touch,
And I see society watching my every move . . .

Vendy Matharu

LETTING GO OF CONFUSION

I've had enough of danger, the pain it's causing me.
No-one knows, no-one else can see.
We're playing the secret lover's game.
But I'm for real, hoping you feel the same.
My feeling's getting stronger, I love you so.
I can't help it, I just can't let go.

We've broken all the rules, never giving up.
The things that matter, all corrupt.
Gaining nothing, always losing out.
Frustration yearning, is this what it's all about?
We'll never be together, I think you know,
But I can't help it, I can't let go.

Lies and secrets is all we ever say and do,
I try and put the blame on no-one else but you.
But the times together are so much fun.
We make each other shine, shine like the sun.
The future could be ours, but we'll never know,
At the moment though, I really can't let go.

Fools in love is all we are,
Things should have never got this far.
My heart's hurting, feel it breaking,
Confused, I can't go on waiting.
If you really love me, then let me know,
But if you don't, just let me go.

Annette Willsher

THE FOREGROUND OF LONELINESS

In the foreground of this loneliness
A sick wind rattles the loose pane,
Which taps impatiently -
Eager for release.

Long away I watch a motor slip
Through a streamed and wooded landscape,
On to which a summer pours
Burning shades.

And now a rushing wind occurs
Which flings the curtain at my face,
Smothering me like
Polythene.

In these few moments I am blind once more,
Unborn in the musty wrap of curtain,
With only the wind's tap-tap
Dancing on the pane.

Dominic Allard

PREY

Exchanging anxious glances
in we trundle
Forcing smiles for Gran
a sad little bundle
With her face
of black and purple.
Father mutters . . . police . . .
bloody delays . . .
I'll make sure the
bastard mugger pays
I shall pray
for him she says.

Edward Wood

WINDS OF CHANGE

An English rose, an English garden
This haven is my home
As I wandered down my garden path
I saw a little gnome.

What is the matter my little friend
You look so tired and sad
You have walked this land one hundred years
What on earth could be so bad.

He took the robin to his shoulder
And gently held my hand
My story is short, but sad to me
The winds of change run through our land.

Once there were birds, too many to count
Now thick with oil their time running out
The whales and the dolphins who once swam free
Now swim murky waters unable to see
The rain forests thick with fruits and seeds
Now thinned every second to pamper man's greed
The lions and tigers once dreamed under trees
Now sit in their cages and long to be free.

A silence of shame came over my garden
This haven I call my home
he gave me a rose, the thorn cut deeply
Now learn, said my little gnome.

A rose is a rose, but you are the thorn
A forest a forest, but you let it die
A bird is a bird, but you built the cage
A tear is a tear, and you made me cry.

Maureen Gentry-Evans

THE COLD'S NOT WHAT IT SEEMS

So where are they now?
As the winter lays her song.
Drag up the shawl
Bitter shoulders don't belong.

The pictures flicker on
As the flames begin to die
And the face that loves
Turns ragged and slowly starts to cry.

What is the cold?
That beats often at the door.
Where is the loneliness?
To return and grieve once more.

The times have not been lost
They're there in eyes of old.
The love, the caring breast
Still keeps us from the cold.

Then why do we ache
To see the winter fall?
The best has not gone by
It is there for us to call.

So sleep within your winter
And the fiery pictures of your dreams.
Keep the night outside your heart
For the cold's not what it seems.

A J Lewis

UNTITLED

Around this doorway gathered
We watch one of us pass through,
Into what room, it's hard to say -
Perhaps one of wood, encased in clay.

Or perhaps into a white room
Where there's chicken every day -
Served in white wine sauce again
And on a silver tray.

Or maybe into a forest -
Dense and full of flowers
Where the grass will serve as paving
And the trees as stately towers.

But then it might be home -
Just as we recall
With dinner in the oven
And wet winter coats in the hall.

C Martin

SEPARATION

I remember the last fading dawn,
In my memory as if it were only yesterday.
Shards of light pierce through the once dark forest,
Colours of unimaginable radiance,
Ranging from one end of the spectrum to the opposite,
Green plant life soaking up the sun's rays,
Now in darkness shadows do I only walk,
Destruction of something so beautiful tortures me,
I admire all the beauty within my demon realm,
It is the only home I know.

Noel James Gillham

THE BOX

I crawl into my box
To avoid the teeth of the fox.
I close tightly the lid and I know I have hid
My face from decision with careful precision.
In my box I'm protected
I know I've defected
From life and the choice, but I still hear the voice
That shouts in my mind; 'There is something to find.'
Outside the fox prowls.
'Fight me,' it howls.
So I lift off the lid and I make a last bid
For a life that is me.
Will the fox let me be?

Jo Gray

FLICKERING SHADOW

Flickering shadow, dancing across the hall.
Into the bedroom and under the bed,
Then out through the wall.

Folding stretching shrinking turning.
There seems to be no limit to your form.
Up onto the ceiling, then down onto the floor
Quite suddenly you disappear, I turn and you are reborn

Yet, who is this other person?
This other me, that dares to imitate my every move
With a mere parody.

But this darkened patch of anti light
Shows a remarkable resistance
That brings a comfort to my soul
For it serves as confirmation of my own existence.

Floyd Coggins

RESTITUTION

Trembling and fearful for past wrongs repeated,
Raised expectations to challenge our fears;
Turning the tide from resentment and hatred,
Transfiguration from anger and tears.
Fight for our freedom, our heart and our history,
Restore our land and our living beside;
Honing the roughness and polishing our purpose,
Claiming inheritance, language and pride.
Exiles and prodigals, slowly returning
Over the border that kept us apart,
Bring new ideals with a life for the future
Food for our souls and a fragile new start.

How can we justify past degradation?
Pits closed in poverty; mines worked in blood;
Townships and villages filled with our grieving;
Bricks build from squalor with sweat and with mud;
Coal, diamonds, slate - all were bought with our suffering;
Gold grasped from slavery, bodies bowed low.
Make reparation; reach out for forgiveness;
Offer atonement; let seeds start to grow.

Feel the earth warming, expanding, enveloping
All who aspire to an aim that is just.
Look to the future with anticipation,
Countries in blossom return from the dust,
Bringing the day of the true revelation
Ordered by God for a time yet to come,
Prophesied, mystical, anxiously hoped for
Coming millennium, spiritual home.

Penny Leigh-Brown

NEW LIFE

She was so beautiful
See her tiny hands and feet
With hands like his
And eyes like mine
Then she cried
And I sang lullabies
peaceful sleep
Slumber deep
Don't weep
She looked so sweet
We felt so complete
A happy family
But was it meant to be
Forever
That we'd stay together
Birds flee the nest
And stay away
They make their way
And find another place to rest
But it's not the same for us
We should still be
In touch
We still need love
From our mothers, fathers
Sisters and brothers
And not be apart
From one another
Forever

Kathryn Longley

DREAM MAKER

He caresses her with words in rhyme
Like fingers running down her spine.
Gently, softly, touching her
He makes love with spoken word.

He brings her dreams and stirrings deep
Into her thoughts for her to keep.
Of castles and their knights so brave,
In shining armour, their maid to save.

Riding cross country on a steed of white,
To darken countries a dragon to fight.
The lady she doth wait for him,
To slay the dragon; her freedom to win.

The Dream Maker he brought her light,
Into the deepest, darkest night.
And left her with the memories deep,
Of caresses softly in her sleep.

Of firelight dancing in the night,
The red and orange and yellow so bright.
Licking over shoulders bare,
Passionate thoughts without a care.

But as the grey of dawn sets in,
She wakens from the dream within,
To cold and heavy light of day,
Her dream for warmth, come what may!

Debbie Benton

UNTITLED

My keep fit class are all over 50
Everyone is surprisingly nifty
We're up on the step and down on the floor
Come on shouts Barbara, give me two more

She's 55 and slim and lithe
A lovely sight for anyone's eyes

She never gets tired, she never gets blue
Come on ladies, it's good for you

Your bones will get stronger
You'll all live longer
Your tummies get flatter, it really does matter

Your bums will be firmer, your thighs will shrink
When I've finished with you, you'll be in the pink

Our Xmas night out was quite a rave
A demonstration of aerobics we gave

The waitress said, you're a lively crowd
Come on over 50's you can all be proud

Join a keep fit class and pound away
In six months' time you'll be able to say

I'm slimmer and fitter and healthier too
Your family will be proud of you

Chrissy Thompson

INFORMATION

We hope you have enjoyed reading this book - and that you will continue to enjoy it in the coming years.

If you like reading and writing poetry drop us a line, or give us a call, and we'll send you a free information pack.

Write to

Poetry Now Information
1-2 Wainman Road
Woodston
Peterborough
PE2 7BU